essentials
children's
KNITS

First published in Great Britain in 1993
by Hamlyn, an imprint of Reed Consumer Books Limited
Michelin House, 81 Fulham Road, London SW3 6RB
and Auckland, Melbourne, Singapore and Toronto

Copyright © 1993 IPC Magazines

ISBN 0 600 57831 3

A catalogue record for this book is available at the British Library

Produced by Mandarin Offset
Printed and bound in Hong Kong

ACKNOWLEDGEMENTS

Editor: Carolyn Price
Design: Town Group Consultancy, London.
Production: Fiona Wright
These patterns have all appeared in *Essentials*, *Me* or *Essentials Kids' Knits*

Photographs: Sandra Lousada, Sarah Hutchings, Belinda Banks, Nigel Limb,
Mike Van Der Vord, Chris Edwick, Alex Lawson-Thomas, Wendy Carrig,
Liz McAulay, Gerald Wortman, Fiona Pragoff, Peter Waldman, Di Lewis, Pia Tryde,
Toni Revan, Tony Boase.

With thanks to: Gail Abbott, Melody Griffiths, Sue Horan, Jane Binsley.

CONTENTS

babies' and toddlers' knits

Bobble and Leaf Pattern Top and Pants 6
Stripey Playsuit 8
Colourful Matching Set 10
Snowman Sweater 12
Button Neck Aran 14
Top to Toe 16
Bunny Dress 18
First Christmas 20
Peruvian Sweater and Hat 22
Dungaree Outfit 24
Cricket Cardigan 26
Frilled Top and Trousers 28
Baby Layette 30

classic knits

Snowflake Pattern Sweater and Beret 34
Cable Dress and Leg Warmers 36
Aran Sweater 38
School Button-Neck Pullover 40
Spanish Bolero 42
Striped V-Neck Sweater 44
Boys' Slipover 46
Rope Cable Cardigan 48
Kids' Jacket and Beret 50
Fair Isle Sweater 52
Girls' Summer Cardigan 54
Classic Cricket Sweater 56
Bright Summer Sweater 58
Winter Warmers 60
Duffle Coat 62
Traditional Fair Isle Sweater and Hat 64

patterned knits

Pierrot Sweater and Cropped Pants 68
Scottie Dog Sweater and Beret 70
Geometric Cardigan 72
Colourful Cardigan 74
Zig Zag Fair Isle 76
Teddy Bear Sweater 78
Bow Sweater 80
Baseball Jacket 82
Alpine Daisy Cardigan 84
Contrast Cardigan 86
Goosey Goosey Gander Sweater 88
Sailor Suits 90
Clown Face Sweater 92
Christmas Holly Sweater 94

Knitters' Notes

TENSION

It's always tempting to skip this bit and go straight into the pattern, but getting the tension right can make the difference between a knit that fits and one that ends up looking like your kids are wearing someone else's clothes!

The needle sizes we recommend throughout this book are the ones that the pattern designers used to get the tension given in the instructions, but you may find you need a different size needle to obtain the same tension. When you make your test square, you should experiment with different needle sizes until you get the same number of stitches and rows to the given measurement as the pattern. Even if you're an experienced knitter, you should test your tension for every new pattern – a new yarn, an unfamiliar technique, even a change of mood can affect your tension.

Start with the needle size given. Cast on a few more stitches than given for the tension and work a few extra rows – edge stitches can be hard to measure. Work in the stitch given as tension is not always measured over stocking stitch.

When you've completed the square, press it if necessary then lay it out on a flat surface. Count out the number of stitches given for the tension and mark with pins, then measure the distance between them. If you get the correct measurement, you can be sure that your finished garment will be the right size. If it measures less than is required, your knitting is too tight and the garment will knit up small, so try again using larger needles. If it measures more than is required your knitting is too loose, so try again using a smaller size needle.

If you do need to use a different size of needle for your garment, don't forget to change the other needle sizes given in the pattern.

SIZES

All our patterns give the actual finished measurements of the garment, as well as a 'to fit chest' size. Depending on the style, there'll be a different amount of 'ease' allowed in the pattern. If in doubt make a bigger size – children grow!

ABBREVIATIONS

( ) figures in round brackets refer to larger sizes; where there is only one set of figures, it applies to all sizes.
[] work instructions in square brackets as directed.
Any special abbreviations are shown at start of each pattern.
alt = alternate
beg = beginning
CH = chain
cm = centimetre(s)
cont = continue(ing)
DC = double crochet
dec = decrease(ing)
foll = following
g st = garter stitch (knit every row)
in = inches
inc = increase(ing)
K = knit
K up = pick up and knit
M1 = make one stitch by picking up loop lying between needles and knitting into the back of it
m st = moss stitch
P = purl
patt = pattern
psso = pass slipped stitch over
rem = remain(ing)
rep = repeat
rev = reverse
RS = right side
skpo = slip one stitch, K1, pass slipped st over
sl = slip
ss = slip stitch
st(s) = stitch(es)
st st = stocking stitch (K1 row, P1 row)
tbl = through back of loop
tog = together
WS = wrong side
yo = yarn over
yon = yarn over needle
yfwd = yarn forward
yrh = yarn round hook

PRESSING

It's a good idea to keep a ball band in a safe place for guidance on pressing and washing the garment.

KNITTING NEEDLE SIZES

UK	METRIC	CANADA
0	8mm	11
1	7½mm	–
2	7mm	–
3	6½mm	10½
4	6mm	10
5	5½mm	9
6	5mm	8
7	4½mm	7
8	4 mm	6
9	3¾mm	5
10	3¼mm	3
11	3mm	–
12	2¾mm	2
13	2¼mm	1
14	2mm	0

CHOOSING YOUR YARN

To give you a greater choice of yarn, for each design we give the yarn thickness and also the fibre content. We also include the yarn in which the original garment was knitted.

The golden rule when buying yarn is to choose one which will knit to the tension of the pattern. Most DK yarns vary only slightly in thickness so it should be possible to choose from a wide range of yarns.

Be guided by the fibre content in the pattern noting that in general natural fibre yarns e.g. pure wool or pure cotton, have a shorter yardage per ball than 100% synthetic yarns. If substituting a wool or cotton yarn for a synthetic yarn it may be necessary to buy extra balls. Similarly if you replace a wool or cotton yarn with a synthetic yarn you may require fewer balls. If in doubt your wool shop will be happy to help. They may provide a lay-by service where the yarn can be held on one side to be purchased a few balls at a time, as and when required.

MEASUREMENTS

All measurements on diagrams are given in centimetres.

babies' and toddlers' **KNITS**

Bobble and Leaf Pattern Top and Pants

The pattern panels on this top and pants are knitted in a bobble and leaf design, with embroidered flowers worked afterwards.

Skill Rating Experienced
Sizes To fit age 3(6) months
Top To fit chest 18(20)in/46(51)cm *Actual size* 56(63)cm
Length 26(34)cm *Sleeve seam* 18(26)cm
Pants: Length 35(42.5)cm *Hip* 50(55)cm
Materials Top and Pants 6(7) x 50g balls of 45% acrylic/40% nylon/15% wool DK in cream and small amounts same in royal blue, yellow and green for embroidery
We used Patons Beehive DK
Pair each of 3¼mm and 4mm knitting needles
Waist length of 1cm wide elastic • Cable needle
Tension 27 sts and 31 rows to 10cm over patt on 4mm needles

Special Abbreviations

C2B = sl next 2 sts onto cable needle, hold at back, K2b, K2b from cable needle
C2F = sl next 2 sts onto cable needle, hold in front, K2b, K2b from cable needle
K1b = knit into back of stitch
MB = make bobble by working K1, yo, K1, yo, K1 all into one st, turn, P5, turn, K3 tog, K2 tog, pass first stitch over second
M1p = make one by purling into front and back of stitch
P1b = purl into back of stitch

TOP

BACK

Using 3¼mm needles, cast on 77(87)sts.
1st rib row (RS) K1b, [P1, K1b] to end.
2nd rib row P1b, [K1, P1b] to end. Rep these 2 rows for 3cm, ending with a 2nd rib row. Change to 4mm needles and cont from chart. **1st row** (RS) K2(5) sts, * reading row 1 from right to left, work 23 sts of chart, K2(4) sts, rep from * twice, K0(1) st. **2nd row** K2(5) sts, * reading row 2 from left to right, work 23 sts of chart, K2(4) sts, rep from * twice, K0(1) st. Beg with 3rd row of chart, cont in this way, working g st as set until 72(96) patt rows have been completed. Cast off loosely.

FRONT

Work as given for back until 48(72) patt rows have been completed.
Shape neck **Next row** (RS) Patt 27(29) sts, turn. Cont on these sts only for 1st side and leave rem sts on a spare needle. Cont straight in patt as set until front matches back to shoulder. Cast off.
With RS of work facing sl centre 23(29) sts onto a holder, rejoin yarn to inner end of rem sts and patt to end. Complete to match 1st side.

SLEEVES

Using 3¼mm needles, cast on 37(41) sts. Work 3cm K1b, P1 twisted rib as given for back. Change to 4mm needles and cont from chart: **1st row** K7(9), work 1st row of chart, K7(9) sts. **2nd row** K7(9), work 2nd row of chart, K7(9) sts. Beg with 3rd row of chart, cont as set and inc one st at each end of 5th and every foll 6th row, taking inc sts into g st, until there are 49(59) sts. Cont straight until 48(72) chart rows have been completed. Cast off.

COLLAR

Join shoulder seams. Using 4mm needles, and with RS of work facing, K23(29) centre front sts from holder. Cont in g st until collar edge fits around three sides of neck opening. Cast off loosely.

TO MAKE UP

Do not press. Taking care not to sew tightly, join right edge of collar to right side of neck for a girl and left edge of collar to left edge for a boy. Sl stitch cast off edge of collar loosely on WS and turn collar back. Place markers 11(13.5)cm down from shoulders on back and front. Sew in sleeves between markers.
Embroider as photograph on page 5 (royal blue for lazy daisy flowers, yellow for French knot flower centres and green for detached chain st leaves). Join side and sleeve seams.

PANTS

SIDE PANELS

Make 2 Using 4mm needles cast on 25 sts. K1 row. Cont from chart: **1st row** (RS) K1, reading row 1 from right to left work 23 sts of chart, K1. **2nd row** K1, reading row 2 from left to right work 23 sts of chart, K1. Beg with 3rd row of chart cont as set until 96(120) chart rows are worked. Cast off.

RIGHT LEG

Using 4mm needles cast on 54(60) sts. K 48(62) rows.
Shape crotch **Next row** (RS) K25(28), turn. Cont on these sts only for 1st side and leave rem sts on a spare needle. Cont in g st, dec one st at inner edge on every foll alt row until 22(25) sts rem. Leave sts on a holder. Rejoin yarn to inner end of rem sts, cast off 4 sts and K to end. Complete to match first side.

LEFT LEG

Work as given for right leg.

BACK

Placing centre cast off sts of each leg tog for crotch, using 4mm needles K across 22(25) sts of back right leg and 22(25) sts of back left leg. 44(50) sts. Cont straight in g st until side edges match length of side panels. Leave sts on a holder.

FRONT

Work as given for back.

FRONT WAISTBAND

Join side panels to side edges of front. Using 3¼mm needles K up 25 sts across side panel, K across stitches on holder inc one st at centre, K up 25 sts across side panel. 95(101) sts. Work 14 rows K1b, P1 twisted rib as given for back of top. Cast off loosely in rib.

BACK WAISTBAND

Work as given for front waistband across sts on holder only.

ANKLE CUFFS

Making 2 pleats at back and 3 pleats at front and picking up through all layers of g st, using 3¼mm needles K up 13 sts from side panel and 28(34) sts from pleated g st. 41(47) sts. Work 10 rows K1b, P1 twisted rib. Cast off in rib.

TO MAKE UP

Join cuff, side, crotch and waistband seams. Embroider motifs on side panels as for top. Fold waistband in half to WS and catch st leaving a gap. Thread waist elastic, join ends and close gap.

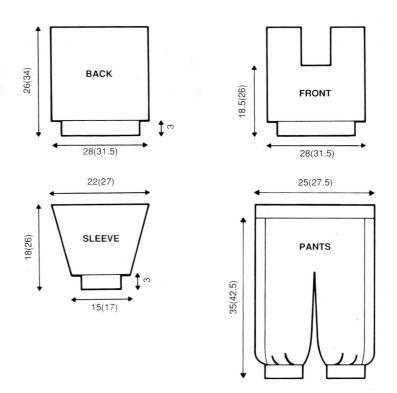

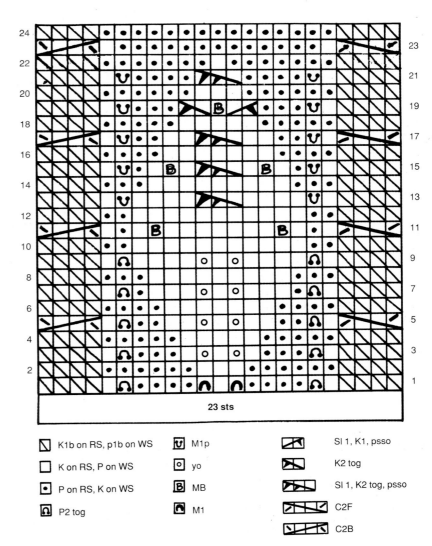

◻ K1b on RS, p1b on WS	⋃ M1p
◻ K on RS, P on WS	◯ yo
◻ P on RS, K on WS	B MB
⌒ P2 tog	⋒ M1

Sl 1, K1, psso

K2 tog

Sl 1, K2 tog, psso

C2F

C2B

Stripey Playsuit

Don't throw away those odd bits of wool – they can all add up to this cuddly playsuit and hat.

Skill Rating Easy
Sizes To fit age 6(12) months
Actual chest measurement 51(60.5)cm
Length from shoulder to ankle 56.5(64.5)cm *Sleeve seam* 23(27cm)
Materials Playsuit Approximately 270(300)g of DK wool, including 130(150)g of main colour (colour M) used for edgings
Hat Approximately 40(50)g of DK wool including 10(15)g of main colour (M) used for edgings
Pair each 3¼mm and 4mm knitting needles
6 buttons for playsuit
Tension 22 sts and 28 rows to 10cm over st st on 4mm needles
Note: The set pictured is worked in a stripe sequence of 1 row M and 4 rows contrast, 1 row M and 2 rows contrast. Our instructions, however, are given without reference to stripe pattern so the stripe sequence can be varied according to your choice. You can make the playsuit and hat from any DK yarn as long as you work to the tension given. Sort out lots of colours, the brighter the better, or choose shades of one colour. Make sure that the yarns you've chosen can all be washed in the same way. Then, before you start the pattern, knit some sample squares to create a stripe sequence you like and, of course, to check your tension.

PLAYSUIT

LEFT LEG

Using 3¼ mm needles and M, cast on 39(43)sts. **1st rib row** (RS) K1, [P1, K1] to end. **2nd rib row** (WS) P1, [K1, P1] to end. Rep these 2 rows until work measures 4cm, ending with a 2nd rib row. Change to 4mm needles and cont in st st and stripe pattern, inc one st each end of 11th and every foll alt row until there are 79(91) sts. Work straight until left leg measures 24(27)cm from beg, ending with a WS row.
Shape crotch Cast off 8(9) sts at beg of next row and 2(3) sts at beg of foll row. Dec one st each end of next and every foll alt row until 59(69) sts rem. P 1 row, so ending with a WS row **. Leave sts on a holder.

RIGHT LEG

Work as left leg to crotch shaping.
Shape crotch Cast off 2(3) sts at beg of next row and 8(9) sts at beg of foll row. Complete as left leg crotch to **.
Join legs **Next row** With RS of right leg facing, cast off 2 sts for front opening, K to last st, with RS of left leg facing, K last st of right leg tog with first st of left leg, K to end. 115(135) sts. **Next row** Cast off 2 sts for front opening, P to end. 113(133)

sts. Work straight until playsuit measures 48(54)cm from beg, ending with a WS row.
Divide for armholes **Next row** K24(28), turn and leave rem sts on a spare needle. Cont on these sts for right front, work straight until armhole measures 7(8.5)cm from beg of shaping, ending with a WS row.
Shape neck Cast off 6 sts at beg of next row. Dec one st at neck edge on every row until 14(16) sts rem. Work 5 rows, ending with a WS row. Cast off. With RS facing, rejoin yarn and cast off 5(7) sts then K until there are 55(63) sts on right needle, turn and leave rem sts on a spare needle. Cont on these sts for back, work straight until back matches front to shoulder, ending with a WS row. Cast off. With RS facing, rejoin yarn and cast off 5(7) sts, K to end. 24(28) sts. Work left front to match right front, reversing shapings.

SLEEVES

Using 3¼ mm needles and M, cast on 27(31) sts. Rib 4cm as given for left leg, ending with a 2nd rib row. Change to 4mm needles. Cont in st st inc one st each end of 3rd and every foll 3rd(4th) row until there are 53(57) sts. Work straight until sleeve measures 25(29)cm from beg, ending with a WS row. Cast off.

NECKBAND

Join shoulder seams. Using 3¼mm needles and M with RS facing, K up 14(16) sts up right front neck, 29(33) sts across back neck and 14(16) sts down left front neck. 57(65) sts. **1st rib row** (WS) K1, [P1, K1] to end. **2nd rib row** P1, [K1, P1] to end. Work these 2 rows twice more, work 1st rib row again. Cast off in rib.

BUTTON BAND

Reversing first 2cm of cuff seam, join inner leg seams, then join crotch seam from back to beg of front opening. With 3¼mm needles and M, cast on 7 sts. Cont in g st until button band, slightly stretched, fits up front opening to top of neckband. Cast off. Sew on the band. Mark 6 button positions on the band, the first one 5.5cm from cast-on edge, the top one 1cm from cast-off edge and the others spaced evenly in between.

BUTTONHOLE BAND

Work as for button band making buttonholes to correspond with markers as follows: **Buttonhole row** K3, yfwd,K2 tog, K2.

TO MAKE-UP

Join cast-off edges of sleeves to row ends of armholes, then join row ends at tops of sleeves to cast-off edges of armholes, ending at centre of underarm cast-off edge. Join sleeve seams, reversing first 2cm of cuff seam. Lapping buttonhole band over button band, sew ends of bands in place. Sew on buttons.

HAT

RIGHT FLAP

Using 4mm needles and M, cast on 27(32) sts. K 6 rows ***. **Next row** K to end. **Next row** P to last 5 sts, K5. Work the last 2 rows 4 more times. Cut off yarn and leave sts on a stitch holder.

LEFT FLAP

Work as for right flap to ***. **Next row** K to end. **Next row** K5, P to end. Work these 2 rows 4 more times. **Next row** K to end, turn and using M, cast on 28(38) sts, then with RS facing, K27(32) sts from right flap holder. 82(102) sts. **Next row** P22(27), with M, K38(48), then P22(27). **Next row** K22(27), with M, K38(48), then K22(27). Rep the last 2 rows twice more. Cont in st st until right and left flaps measure 15(15.5)cm from beg, ending with a P row. **1st dec row** K1, [K2 tog, K6(8)] to last 9(11) sts, K2 tog, K7(9). 72(92) sts. **Next and every WS row** P to end. **2nd dec row** K1, [K2 tog, K5(7)] to last 8(10) sts, K2 tog, K6(8). 62(82) sts. **3rd dec row** K1, [K2 tog, K4(6)] to last 7(9) sts, K2 tog, K5(7). 52(72) sts. **4th dec row** K1, [K2 tog, K3(5)] to last 6(8) sts, K2 tog, K4(6). 42(62) sts. **5th dec row** K1, [K2 tog, K2(4)] to last 5(7) sts, K2 tog, K3(5). 32(52) sts. **6th dec row** K1, [K2 tog, K1(3)] to last 4(6) sts, K2 tog, K2(4). 22 (42) sts. *2nd size only* **7th dec row** K1, [K2 tog, K2] to last 5 sts, K2 tog, K3. 32 sts. **8th dec row** K1, [K2 tog, K1] to last 4 sts, K2 tog, K2. 22 sts. *Both sizes* Cut off yarn, thread end through sts, draw up and secure. Sew back seam.

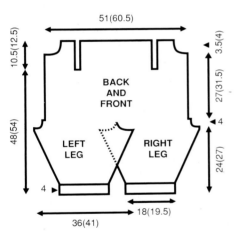

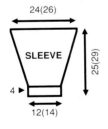

Colourful Matching Set

This matching set in colourful cotton is easy to make and lots of fun for baby to wear.

Skill Rating Easy
Sizes To fit age 9(12) months
Sweater: Actual chest measurement 56(66)cm *Length to shoulder* 21(25)cm
Sleeve seam 18(20)cm *Pants:* Length 30(34)cm
Materials For complete set 2 x 50g balls 100% of cotton DK in red (colour A), 5 balls same in jade (B) and 1 ball same in each of blue (C), peach (D) and pink (E)
We used Hayfield Raw Cotton DK
Pair each of 3¼mm and 4mm knitting needles • 10 small buttons
Tension 22 sts and 30 rows to 10cm over patt on 4mm needles

SWEATER

BACK

Using 3¼mm needles and A, cast on 55(65) sts. Work 7 rows g st. **Inc row** K3(2), *inc in next st, K7(9), rep from * 5 times , inc in next st, K3(2). 62(72) sts. Change to 4mm needles. **1st row** K with B. **2nd row** P with B. **3rd and 4th rows** As 1st and 2nd. **5th row** K with A. **6th row** P with C. **7th row** K2C, [3D, 2C] to end. **8th row** P2C, [3D, 2C] to end. **9th row** As 7th. **10th row** P with C. **11th row** K with A. **12th row** P with B. **13th row** K with B. **14th and 15th rows** As 12th and 13th rows. **16th row** P with A. **17th row** K with E. **18th row** P2E, [3C, 2E] to end. **19th row** K2E, [3C, 2E] to end. **20th row** As 18th. **21st row** K with E. **22nd row** P with A. These 22 rows form patt. Patt straight until back measures 21(25)cm from beg, ending P row.
Shape shoulders Cast off 20(23) sts at beg of next 2 rows. 22(26) sts. Change to 3¼mm needles and A. Work 5 rows g st for neckband. Cast off.

FRONT

Work as given for back until 12 fewer rows have been worked than back to shoulders, ending P row.
Shape neck **Next row** Patt 27(31), turn. Cont on these sts only for 1st side and leave rem sts on spare needle. Keeping patt correct, dec one st at neck edge on next 7(8) rows. 20(23) sts. Patt 4(3) rows, so front matches back to shoulder. Cast off. With RS facing, sl centre 8(10) sts onto a holder, rejoin yarn to inner end of rem sts and patt to end. Complete to match 1st side but patt 1 extra row before casting off.

SLEEVES

Using 3¼mm needles and A, cast on 30(35) sts. Work 5 rows g st. **Inc row** K3, * inc in next st, K3(4), rep from * 5 times, inc in next st, K2(1). 37(42) sts. Change to 4mm needles. Cont in patt as given for back inc one st at each end of 3rd row and every foll 4th row, taking inc sts into patt, until there are 51(60) sts. Patt straight until sleeve measures 18(20)cm from beg, ending P row. Cast off loosely.

FRONT NECKBAND

With RS facing, 3¼mm needles and A, K up 17(20) sts down left front neck, K across 8(10) sts on holder then K up 17(20) sts up right front neck. 42(50) sts. Work 4 rows g st. Cast off.

BUTTONHOLE BANDS

With RS facing, 3¼mm needles and A, K up 24(27) sts evenly across one front shoulder, including ends of neckband. K 2 rows. **Buttonhole row** K3, * yfwd, K2 tog, K6(7), rep from * once, yfwd, K2 tog, K3(4). K 1 row. Cast off. Work other side to match, reversing buttonhole row.

BUTTON BANDS

Work as buttonhole bands, omitting buttonholes.

TO MAKE UP

Lap buttonhole bands over button bands and catch together at shoulder edges. Sew on buttons. Place markers on side edges of back and front 12(14)cm from centre of shoulder bands. Sew on sleeves between markers. Join side and sleeve seams.

PANTS

LEGS

Make 2 Using 3¼mm needles and A, cast on 56(66) sts. Work 7 rows g st. Change to 4mm needles and B, cont in st st with B. Cont straight until work measures 12(14)cm from beg, ending with a P row.
Shape crotch Cast on 3 sts at beg of next 2 rows. Inc one st at each end of 5th and every foll 8th row until there are 68(78) sts. Cont straight until work measures 18(20)cm from beg of shaping, ending with a K row. **Dec row** P1(6), * P2 tog, P5, rep from * 8 times, P2 tog, P2(7). 58(68) sts. Change to 3¼mm needles and A. K 1 row. Work 7 rows K1, P1 rib. Cast off loosely in rib.

STRAPS

Using 3¼mm needles and A, cast on 78(88) sts. Work in g st throughout. K 2 rows. **3rd row** K3, yfwd, K2 tog, K7, turn. **4th row** K12. **5th row** Cast off 12 sts, K to end. **6th row** K to end, cast on 12 sts. **7th row** K12, turn. **8th row** K12. **9th row** K3, yfwd, K2 tog, K to end. **10th row** K to end. **11th row** Cast off 54(64) sts, turn. **12th row** Cast on 54(64) sts. K 2 rows. Rep 3rd to 10th rows once. Cast off all sts.

TO MAKE UP

Join centre front and centre back seams. Join inside leg seams. Sew short, straight end of straps to top of rib at centre back. Sew buttons in pairs to front rib.

HAT

Using 3¼mm needles and A, cast on 86(92) sts. Work 5 rows g st. **Inc row** K5, *inc in next st, K14(8), rep from * 4(8) times, inc in next st, K5. 92(102) sts. Change to 4mm needles and cont in patt as sweater back. Work 1st to 22nd rows, then work 1st and 2nd rows again. Cont in B. **1st dec row** K1, * K2 tog, K7(8), rep from * 9 times, K1. **Next row** P to end. **2nd dec row** K1, * K2 tog, K6(7), rep from * 9 times, K1. **Next row** P to end. **3rd dec row** K1, * K2 tog, K5(6), rep from * 9 times, K1. **Next row** P to end. Cont to dec in this way until 22 sts rem. Break yarn, thread end through rem sts, draw up tightly and secure. Join centre back seam.

SOCKS

Both alike Using 3¼mm needles and A, cast on 32(37) sts. Work 6 rows g st. Change to 4mm needles and cont in patt

as sweater back. Work 1st to 14th rows.
Cont in B.

Shape instep **Next row** K21(25), turn.
Next row P10(13), turn. St st 10(12) rows
on these 10(13) sts, ending with a P row.
Break off yarn and leave sts on a holder.
Next row Place 1st 11(12) sts onto 4mm
needle, then on same needle K up 11(13)
sts along row ends of instep, K across
10(13) sts on holder, K up 11(14) sts along
row-ends of instep then K across rem
11(12) sts. 54(64) sts. Work 7 rows g st.

Shape foot **1st row** [K1, K2 tog,
K21(26), K2 tog, K1] twice. **2nd row** K to
end. **3rd row** [K1, K2 tog, K19(24), K2
tog, K1] twice. **4th row** K to end. **5th row**
[K1, K2 tog, K17(22), K2 tog, K1] twice.
6th row K to end. Cast off rem sts. Join
foot and centre back seam.

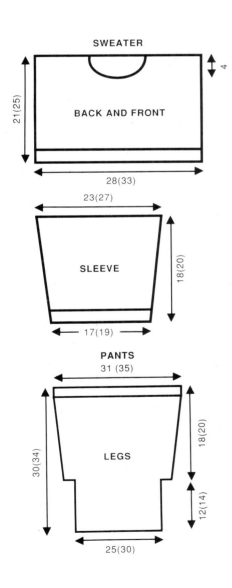

SWEATER

BACK AND FRONT

21(25)

4

28(33)

SLEEVE

23(27)

18(20)

17(19)

PANTS

31 (35)

LEGS

30(34)

18(20)

12(14)

25(30)

Snowman Sweater

A cosy crew-necked sweater knitted in a two-colour Fair Isle pattern.

Skill Rating Medium
Sizes To fit age 1(2:4:6:8:10) years
To fit chest 20(22:24:26:28:30)in/51(56:61:66:71:76)cm
Actual size 64(69:74:78:85:90)cm
Length to shoulder 26(32:38:44:49:52)cm *Sleeve seam* 21(24:27:34:37:41)cm
Materials 4(4:5:5:6:6) x 50g balls of 100% wool DK in
royal blue (colour A) and 1(1:1:1:2:2) balls same in white (B)
We used Emu Superwash DK
Pair each of 3¼mm and 4mm knitting needles
Tension 25 sts and 25 rows to 10cm over patt on 4mm needles

BACK

Using 3¼mm needles and A, cast on 63(67:71:75:81:85) sts. **1st row** (RS) K1, * P1, K1, rep from * to end. **2nd row** P1, * K1, P1, rep from * to end. Rep these 2 rows for 5cm, ending with a 1st row. **Inc row** Rib 8(7:6:5:5:4), * M1, rib 3, rep from * to last 7(6:5:4:4:3) sts, M1, rib to end. 80(86:92:98:106:112) sts. Change to 4mm needles.
Strand yarn not in use loosely across back of work. Reading odd numbered (K) rows from right to left and even numbered (P) rows from left to right, work in patt from chart 1. Rep the 16 patt sts 5(5:5:6:6:7) times across and work first and last 0(3:6:1:5:0) sts as indicated on chart. Cont to work in patt, rep the 18 rows until back measures 26(32:38:44:49:52)cm, ending with a WS row.
Shape shoulders Cast off 9(10:10: 11:12:12) sts at beg of next 4 rows and 9(9:11:11:11:13) sts at beg of foll 2 rows. Cut off yarn and leave rem 26(28:30: 32:36:38) sts on a holder.

FRONT

Work as given for back until front measures 22(27:33:38:43:46)cm from beg, ending with a WS row.
Shape neck **Next row** Patt 34(36:38: 41:45:47), turn and leave rem sts on a spare needle. Cont on these sts dec one st at neck edge on every row until 27(29:31: 33:35:37) sts rem. Cont without shaping until front measures same as back to shoulders, ending at side edge.
Shape shoulder Cast off 9(10:10:11:12: 12) sts at beg of next and foll alt row. Patt 1 row, then cast off rem 9(9:11:11:11:13) sts. Return to sts on spare needle. With RS facing, slip first 12(14:16:16:16:18) sts on to a holder, join yarns to next st and patt to end of row. Complete to match other side of neck reversing shapings.

SLEEVES

Using 3¼mm needles and A, cast on 33 (35:37:39:39:41) sts and work 5cm in K1, P1 rib, as given for back, ending with a 1st row. **Inc row** Rib 3(6:7:5:2:6), * M1, rib 2(2:2:3:3:3), rep from * to last 2(5:6:4:1:5) sts, M1, rib to end. 48(48:50:50:52:52) sts. Change to 4mm needles and work in patt from chart 2 as indicated. Rep the 16 patt sts 3 times across and work first and last 0(0:1:1:2:2) sts as indicated, at the same time, inc and work into patt one st at each end of every foll 3rd row until row 18 has been completed. Cont to work from chart, inc one st at each end of every 3rd row until there are 72(78:84:90:96:102) sts. Cont without shaping until sleeve measures 21(24:27:34:37:41)cm from beg, ending with a WS row. Cast off loosely.

NECKBAND

Join right shoulder seam. With RS facing, 4mm needles and A, K up 16(18:18: 22:22:22) sts down left side of neck, inc one st at each end, K sts from holder, K up 16(18:18:22:22:22) sts up right side of neck, then inc 3 sts evenly across K sts from holder. 75(83:87:97:101:105) sts. Work 7(7:8:8:9:9)cm in rib. Cast off loosely in rib.

TO MAKE UP

Join left shoulder and neckband seam reversing half the neckband seam for foldover section. Mark position of underarms 14.5(15.5:17:18:19:20.5)cm down from shoulders on back and front. Sew in sleeves between markers, placing centre of sleeves to shoulder seam. Join side and sleeve seams. Fold neckband in half to RS and turning cast off edge under sew in place using a loose slipstitch.

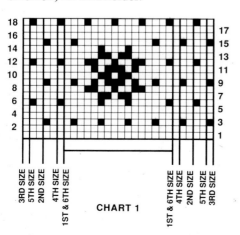

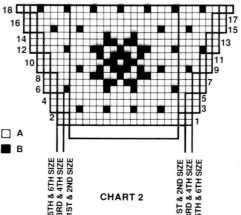

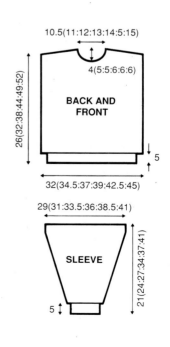

Button Neck Aran

A cabled sweater with clusters of bobbles. The front buttoning collar opens wide to slip easily over baby's head.

Skill Rating Experienced
Sizes To fit age 3 months (6 months:12 months:2 years:4 years)
To fit chest 16(18:20:22:24)in/41(46:51:56:61)cm
Actual size 46(51:56:61:66)cm.
Length to shoulder 26(28:31:35:40)cm *Sleeve seam* 15(18:24:27:31)cm
Materials 4(5:5:6:6) x 50g balls of 100% wool DK in yellow
We used Emu Superwash DK
Pair each 3¼mm and 4mm knitting needles • Cable needle,
3mm crochet hook • 2 buttons
Tension 22 sts and 30 rows to 10cm over st st on 4mm needles
Special Abbreviations
C6B = slip next 3 sts onto cable needle and
leave at back of work, K3, then K3 from cable needle
MB = make bobble: K1, P1, K1, P1 all in next st, turn,
K4, turn, P4, turn, [K2 tog] twice, turn, K2 tog
TW2L = P into back of 2nd st on left needle then K into
front of first st, slip both sts off left needle
TW2R = K into front of 2nd st on left needle then P first st,
slip both sts off left needle

PANEL A

Worked over 13 sts. **1st row** (RS) P13. **2nd row** K13. **3rd row** P6, MB, P6. **4th row** K6,P1,K6. **5th row** P4, MB, P1, K1, P1,MB, P4. **6th row** K4, [P1, K1] twice, P1, K4. **7th row** P2, MB, [P1, K1] 3 times, P1, MB, P2. **8th row** K2, [P1, K1] 5 times, K1. **9th row** P2, [TW2L] twice, K1, [TW2R] twice, P2. **10th row** K3, P1, K1, P3, K1, P1, K3. **11th row** P3, TW2L, M1, sl 1, K2 tog, psso, M1, TW2R, P3. **12th row** K4, P5, K4. **13th row** P4, TW2L, K1, TW2R, P4. **14th row** K5, P3, K5. **15th row** P5, M1, sl 1, K2 tog, psso, M1, P5. **16th row** K6, P1, K6. **17th row** P13. **18th row** K13. These 18 rows form patt for panel A.

PANEL B

Worked over 18 sts. **1st row** (RS) P2, [K6, P2] twice. **2nd and every alt row** K2, [P6, K2] twice. **3rd row** P2, [C6B, P2] twice. **5th row** As 1st. **7th row** As 1st. **8th row** As 2nd. These 8 rows form patt for panel B.

PANEL C

Worked over 6(10:18:18:26) sts. **1st row** (RS) K2,[P2, K2] 1(2:4:4:6) times. **2nd row** P2, [K2, P2] 1(2:4:4:6) times. **3rd row** As 2nd. **4th row** As 1st. These 4 rows form patt for panel C.

BACK

Using 3¼mm needles cast on 48(54:54: 60:66) sts. **1st and every rib row** [K1, P1] to end. Rep this row for 3(3:4:4:5)cm, ending with a RS row. **Next row** Rib 5(8:2:5:8), [inc in next st, rib 1] 19(19: 25:25:25) times, inc in next st, rib 4(7:1: 4:7). 68(74:80:86:92) sts. Change to 4mm needles. Cont in patt: **1st row** (RS) P 0(1: 0:3:2), patt 1st row of each of panels A, B, C, B and A, P 0(1:0:3:2). **2nd row** K 0(1:0: 3:2), patt 2nd row of each of panels A, B, C, B and A, K 0(1:0:3:2). These 2 rows set position of panels. Beg with 3rd row of each panel, cont in patt until back measures 26(28:31:35:40)cm, ending WS row.
Shape shoulders Cast off 12(13:14:15:16) sts at beg of next 4 rows. Cast off rem sts.

FRONT

Work as given for back until front measures 16(17:20:24:28)cm, ending with a WS row.
Shape neck **Next row** Patt 34(37:40: 43:46), turn. Cont on these sts only and leave rem sts on a spare needle. Dec one st at neck edge on next and every foll alt row until 24(26:28:30:32) sts rem. Patt straight until front matches back to shoulder.
Shape shoulder (RS) Cast off 12(13:14: 15:16) sts at beg of next row. Patt 1 row.

Cast off. With RS facing, rejoin yarn to inner end of rem sts, complete to match first side.

SLEEVES

Using 3¼mm needles cast on 28(30:34: 36:42) sts. Work in K1, P1 rib for 2(2:3: 3:3)cm. **Next row** Rib 4(5:7:8:11), inc in each of next 20 sts, rib 4(5:7:8:11). 48(50:54:56:62) sts. Change to 4mm needles. Cont in patt: **1st row** (RS) P3(2:0:1:0), patt 1st row of each of panels B, C and B, P3(2:0:1:0). **2nd row** K3(2:0:1:0), patt 2nd row of each of panels B, C and B, K3(2:0:1:0). These 2 rows set position of panels. Beg with 3rd row of each panel, cont in patt inc one st at each end of next and every foll 5th(5th: 6th:6th:8th) row, working inc sts in rev st st, until there are 62(66:72:76:80) sts. Patt straight until sleeve measures 15(18:24: 27:31)cm from beg, ending with a WS row. Cast off loosely.

COLLAR

Using 3¼mm needles cast on 65(69:75: 81: 85) sts. **1st rib row** K1,[P1, K1] to end. **2nd rib row** P1,[K1, P1] to end. Rep these 2 rows for 3(3:4:4:5)cm, ending with a 2nd rib row.
Divide collar **Next row** Rib 18(19:20: 21: 22), turn. Cont on these sts for front inset leaving rem sts on a spare needle. Dec one st at inner edge on 3rd row and every foll alt row until 2 sts rem. Work 2 tog and fasten off.
Shape back collar **Next row** Rejoin yarn to rem sts, rib 29(31:35:39:41) sts, turn. Cont on these sts for back collar leaving rem sts on spare needle. Rib 1 row. **Next row** Rib 26(28:31:35:37), turn. **Next row** Rib 23(25:27:31:33), turn. **Next row** Rib 20(22:23:27:29), turn. **Next row** Rib 17(19:19:23:25), turn. **Next row** Rib 23(25:27:31:33), turn. Cast off 29(31:35:39:41).
Next row Rejoin yarn to rem sts, rib to end. Complete to match first front inset.

TO MAKE UP

Join shoulder seams. Sew in collar and front insets. Place markers 11(12:13:14:15) cm down from shoulders on back and front. Sew in sleeves between markers. Join side and sleeve seams.
Button edging With RS facing and using crochet hook, work 1 row of DC along edge of front inset, from base to fold in collar. Fasten off.
Buttonhole edging Work to match, making two 2CH buttonholes. Sew on buttons.

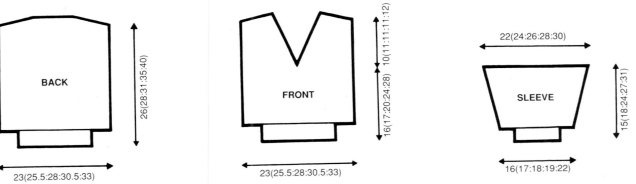

26(28:31:35:40)

BACK

23(25.5:28:30.5:33)

10(11:11:11:12)

16(17:20:24:28)

FRONT

23(25.5:28:30.5:33)

22(24:26:28:30)

15(18:24:27:31)

SLEEVE

16(17:18:19:22)

Top to Toe

Make your baby the best looking tot in town with our easy-knit sweater and pants. Finish with a flourish by adding hat and shoes to match.

Skill Rating Easy
Sizes To fit age 6(12:18) months
Sweater: Actual chest measurement 60(67:73)cm
Length to shoulder 19(22:25)cm *Sleeve seam* 12(14:16)cm
Pants: Length with cuff turned up 29(33:37)cm
Materials Sweater 2 x 50g balls of 60% cotton/40% acrylic DK in green
(colour A) and 2 balls same in pink (B)
Pants 2 balls same in each of A and B
Hat 1 ball same in A *Shoes* 1 ball same in A
We used Pingouin Corrida 4
Pair each of 3¼mm and 4mm knitting needles
Set of 4 double-pointed 3¼mm needles
4mm crochet hook • 1 button for sweater
2 buttons for shoes • Waist length of 1cm wide elastic for pants
Tension 18 sts and 36 rows to 10cm over g st on 4mm needles

SWEATER

BACK

Using 4mm needles and A, cast on 54(60:66) sts. Work 6 rows in g st. Noting that the 1st row will be a RS row, cont in g st stripe patt of 8 rows B and 8 rows A until back measures 10(12:14)cm from beg, ending with a WS row.

Shape armholes Cast off 3 sts at beg of next 2 rows. 48(54:60) sts. Patt until back measures 15(18:21)cm from beg, ending with a WS row.

Neck opening **Next row** K24(27:30), turn. Cont on these sts only and leave rem sts on a spare needle. Patt straight until back measures 19(22:25)cm from beg, ending at armhole edge.

Shape shoulder Cast off 7(8:9) sts at beg of next row and foll alt row. Work 1 row. Cast off rem 10(11:12) sts. With RS facing rejoin yarn to inner end of sts on spare needle. Complete to match 1st side.

FRONT

Work as back to neck opening, ending with a WS row.

Shape neck **1st row** K18(21:24), turn. Cont on these sts only and leave rem sts on a spare needle. Dec one st at neck edge on every row until 14(16:18) sts rem. Patt straight until front matches back to shoulder, ending at armhole edge.

Shape shoulder Cast off 7(8:9) sts at beg of next row. Work 1 row. Cast off rem

7(8:9) sts. With RS facing rejoin yarn to inner end of rem sts, cast off 12 sts, patt to end. Complete to match 1st side.

SLEEVES

Using 4mm needles and A, cast on 24(28:32) sts. Work 7 rows in g st. Cont in stripe patt as back, inc one st at each end of next row and every foll 8th(10th:12th) row until there are 32(36:40) sts. Patt straight until sleeve measures 14(16:18) cm from beg. Cast off loosely.

TO MAKE UP

Join shoulder seams. Using a 4mm crochet hook and A and with RS facing, work 1 round of double crochet evenly around neck and back opening, making a 3 chain loop at top corner of right back. Sew button to top of left back. Set in sleeves, sewing ends of last 6 rows to cast-off sts of armhole shaping. Join side and sleeve seams.

PANTS

LEGS

Right leg Using 3¼mm needles and A, cast on 28(34:40) sts. Work 8cm in K1, P1 rib. **Inc row** (WS) Rib 1(2:4), [inc in each of next 8(3:2) sts, rib 1] 3(8:12) times. 52(58: 64) sts. Change to 4mm needles. Cont in g st in stripe patt of 16 rows B and 16 rows A, at the same time, inc one st at

each end of every foll 4th(6th:6th) row until there are 64(70:76) sts. Patt straight until work measures 17(20:23)cm from beg, ending with a WS row **. Cut off yarns and leave sts on a spare needle.

Left leg Work as right leg to **. Joining row K across sts of left leg to last 2 sts, K last 2 sts of left leg tog with 1st 2 sts of right leg, K across rem sts of right leg. 125(137:149) sts. K 1 row.

Shape crotch **1st row** Cast off 2 sts, K until there are 57(63:69) sts on needle, sl 1, K2 tog, psso, K next st and mark it with a contrast thread, K3 tog, K to end. **2nd row** Cast off 2 sts, K to end. **3rd row** Sl 1, K1, psso, K to within 2 sts of marked st, sl 1, K1, psso, K marked st, K2 tog, K to last 2 sts, K2 tog. **4th row** K to end. Rep last 2 rows once, then work 3rd row again. 105(117:129) sts. Patt straight until work measures 31(35:39)cm from beg, ending with a WS row.

Shape waist **1st row** K12(14:16), turn. Cont on these sts only and leave rem sts on a spare needle. Cast off 6(7:8) sts at beg of next row. K 1 row. Cast off rem 6(7:8) sts. With RS facing rejoin yarn to inner end of rem sts, cast off 81(89:97) sts, K to end. Complete to match first side.

WAISTBAND

With RS facing, 4mm needles and A, pick up and K 93(105:117) sts evenly around waist. Beg P row, work 9 rows st st. Cast off loosely.

TO MAKE UP

Join inside leg seams. Join centre back seam. Fold waistband in half to WS. Sew waistband loosely in place, leaving a small opening for elastic. Thread elastic through waistband, join ends then close the opening.

HAT

Using 3¼mm needles and A, cast on 90(96:102) sts loosely. Work in K1, P1 rib for 14(15:16)cm.

Shape top **1st row** Rib 2, [sl 1, K2 tog, psso, rib 3] to last 4 sts, sl 1, K2 tog, psso, P1. Rib 5 rows. **7th row** [K1, P3 tog] to end. Rib 3 rows. **11th row** Rib 2(0:2), [sl 1, K2 tog, psso, P1] to end. Rib 1 row. Cut off yarn leaving enough to join seam. Thread end through rem 16(16:18) sts, draw up and secure. Join seam, reversing seam for turn back section.

Make stalk Using 3¼mm needles and A, cast on 8 sts. Work 13 rows in K1, P1 rib. Cast off in rib. Join side edges and sew to top of hat. Turn back brim.

SHOES

Using 3¼mm needles and A, cast on 8(10:12) sts. Work 24(28:32) rows in g st. Cut yarn. Using 3 double-pointed needles and beg at centre of cast-on edge, pick up and K 4(5:6) sts to corner, 14(16:18) sts along side edge, K across 8(10:12) sts on needle, then pick up and K14(16:18) sts along side edge and 4(5:6) sts along remainder of cast-on edge. 44(52:60) sts. Working backwards and forwards in rows, work 11 rows in g st.

Shape work **1st row** K26(31:36), turn. **2nd row** K8(10:12), turn. **3rd row** K7(9:11), K2 tog, turn. **4th row** As 3rd. **5th row** K3(4:5), K2 tog, K2(3:4), K2 tog, turn. **6th row** K6(8:10), K2 tog, turn. **7th row** K2(3:4), K2 tog, K2(3:4), K2 tog, turn. **8th row** K5(7:9), K2 tog, turn. Rep 8th row 8 times but work across all sts on the last row. Cast off all sts.

Make strap Using 4mm needles and A, cast on 17(17:19) sts. K 1 row. **Buttonhole row** K2, K2 tog, yfwd, K to end. K 2 rows. Cast off.

TO MAKE UP

Join centre back seam. Sew on strap and button so that each shoe fastens at outer side.

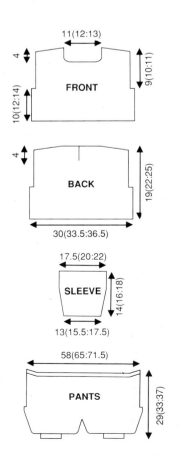

Bunny Dress

A pretty dress with bunnies around the hem and a textured diamond pattern on the bodice and sleeves. The centres of the diamonds are finished with French knots.

Skill Rating Experienced
Sizes To fit age 1(2:4) years
To fit chest 20(22:24)in/51(56:61)cm
Actual size 56(62:66)cm
Length from hem to shoulder 42(46:50)cm *Sleeve seam* 7(8:9)cm
Materials 4(5:5) x 50g balls of 50% Courtelle/40% Bri-Nylon/10% wool DK in white (colour A) and 1 ball same in blue (B)
We used Wendy Family Choice DK
Pair each 3¼mm and 4mm knitting needles • 3 buttons
Tension 24 sts and 32 rows to 10cm over st st on 4mm needles
Special Abbreviations
T2R = K into front of 2nd st on left hand needle, then K first st, slip both sts from needle together
T2L = K into back of 2nd st on left hand needle, then K first st, slip both sts from needle together

BACK

Using 3¼mm needles and A, cast on 127(136:146)sts. Beg with a K row, work 5 rows in st st. **Picot row** [P2 tog, yrn] to last 1(2:2) sts, P1(2:2). Change to 4mm needles. Beg with a K row, work 10 rows in st st. Cont in patt from chart, reading odd-numbered (K) rows from right to left and even-numbered (P) rows from left to right. Use a separate small ball of yarn for each area of colour and twist yarns together when changing colour to avoid a hole. Set chart as folls: with A, K4(0:5), [work 17 sts across 1st row of chart] 7(8:8) times, with A, K to end. Cont in patt as set until 20 rows have been completed. Cont in A only until work measures 26(28: 30)cm from picot row, ending with a P row.
Shape waist **Next row** K4(6:7), [K2 tog] to last 5(6:7) sts, K to end. 68(74:80) sts. **Next row** K to end. **Next row** K1, [yrn, K2 tog] to last st, K1. **Next row** K to end **. Beg with K row, work 12(16:18) rows in st st.
Shape armholes Cast off 3(4:4) sts at beg of next 2 rows. Dec one st at each end of next and every foll alt row until 54(58: 62) sts rem. P1 row.
Divide for opening **Next row** K29(31: 33), turn and cont on these sts only for right back, leaving rem sts on a spare needle. **1st row** (WS) K4, P to end. **2nd row** (RS) K. Rep these 2 rows 4(5:6) more times. **Buttonhole row** K2, yrn, K2 tog, P to end. **Next row** K. Rep rows 1 and 2, 5(6:7) times, work buttonhole row again.

Cont as set for 10(12:14)rows.
Shape shoulder Cast off 11(12:13) sts at beg of next row. Leave rem 18(19:20) sts on a holder.
Left back Using 4mm needles and A, cast on 4 sts, then with RS facing K 25(27:29) sts from spare needle. **Next row** P to last 4 sts, K4. Cont to match right back, reversing shaping and omitting buttonholes.

FRONT

Work as given for back to **.
Commence pattern **1st row** (RS) K 32(35:38), T2R, T2L, K to end. **2nd and every alt row** P. **3rd row** K 30(33:36), [T2R, T2L] twice, K to end. **5th row** K 28(31:34), [T2R, T2L] 3 times, K to end. **7th row** K 28(31:34), [T2L, T2R] 3 times, K to end. **9th row** K 30(33:36), [T2L, T2R] twice, K to end. **11th row** K32(35:38), T2L, T2R, K to end. **12th row** As 2nd row. These 12 rows form diamond patt. Cont in patt work 0(4:6) rows without shaping.
Shape armholes Cont in patt as set, cast off 3(4:4) sts at beg of next 2 rows. Dec one st at each end of next and every foll alt row until 54(58:62) sts rem. Cont without shaping until armholes measure 8(9:10)cm, ending with a WS row.
Shape neck **Next row** K 16(17:18), turn and cont on these sts only for left side of neck, leaving rem sts on a spare needle. Dec one st at neck edge on next 3 rows, then every foll alt row until 11(12:

13) sts rem. Cont without shaping until front measures same as back, ending at armhole edge. Cast off. Sl centre 22(24:26) sts on to a holder, rejoin A and K to end. Complete to match other side of neck.

SLEEVES

Using 3¼mm needles and A, cast on 43 (45:47) sts. Beg with a K row, work 2 rows in st st. **Picot row** [K2 tog, yrn] to last st, K1. **4th row** P to end. **5th row** K to end. **6th row** P into front and back of every st. 86(90:94) sts. Change to 4mm needles.
Commence pattern **1st row** (RS) K 41(43:45), T2R, T2L, K to end. **2nd row** P to end. This sets position of diamond patt. Cont working diamond patt as given for front until sleeve measures 7(8:9)cm from picot row, ending with a P row.
Shape top Cont in patt as set, cast off 3(4:4) sts at beg of next 2 rows, 3(3:4) sts at beg of foll 2 rows, then 2 sts at beg of next 4 rows. Dec one st at each end of next and every foll alt row until 46 sts rem. Work 1 row straight. Cast off 2 sts at beg of next 4 rows, then 4 sts at beg of foll 4 rows. Cast off rem 22 sts.

NECKBAND

Join shoulder seams. Using 3¼mm needles, A and with RS facing, K18(19:20) sts of left back neck, K up 9 sts down left front neck, K 22(24:26) front neck sts, K up 9 sts up right front neck, then K18(19:20) sts of right back neck. 76(80:84) sts. **1st row** K4, P to last 4 sts, K4. **2nd row** K to end. **3rd row** K2, yrn, K2 tog, P to last 4 sts, K4. **4th row** K4, [yrn, K2 tog] to last 4 sts, K4. **5th and 6th rows** As 1st and 2nd rows. **7th row** As 1st row. Cast off loosely.

WAISTCORD

Using 3¼mm needles and A, cast on 210(220:230) sts. K 1 row, then cast off loosely.

TO MAKE UP

Press according to directions on the ball band. Join side seams. Join sleeve seams and sew into armholes, gathering tops of sleeves to fit neatly into armholes.

Turn in all hems to WS on picot row and slip st neatly into place. Sew end of the button band behind buttonhole band at centre back. Sew on buttons. Thread cord through eyelet holes at waist to tie at centre front.

Using B, embroider French knots in diamond pattern on front bodice and sleeves as in photograph.

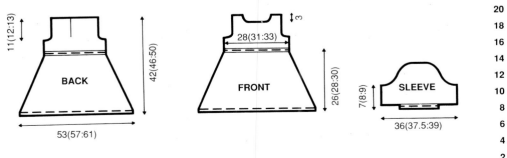

BACK

11(12:13)

42(46:50)

53(57:61)

FRONT

28(31:33)

3

26(28:30)

SLEEVE

7(8:9)

36(37.5:39)

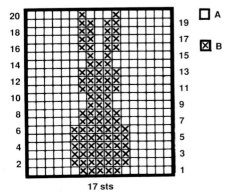

□ A

⊠ B

17 sts

First Christmas

Wrap up your little darling Santa-style for the big day and you'll get a real treat on Christmas morning.

Skill Rating Medium
Sizes Sweater: To fit age 3(6:9:12) months
Actual size 56(61:66:71)cm
Length to shoulder 25(28:33:37)cm *Sleeve seam* 16(17:18:19)cm
Hat and Bootees: To fit age 3-6(9-12) months
Materials 1(1:1:2) x 50g balls of 45% acrylic/40% Bri-Nylon/15% wool DK in white (colour A) and 3(3:3:4) balls in scarlet (B)
One 50g ball 61% acrylic/39% nylon textured DK in white (C)
We used Hayfield Grampian DK and Hayfield Pretty Baby Changes DK
Pair each 3¼mm and 4mm knitting needles
3 buttons and shirring elastic for sweater • Crochet hook
Tension 22 sts and 28 rows to 10cm over st st on 4mm needles

SWEATER

BACK

Using 4mm needles and A, cast on 122 (134:146:158) sts. Work 6 rows g st. Beg with a K row, work 5 rows st st. **Dec row** [P2 tog] to end. 61(67:73:79) sts. Cont in st st from chart stranding colour not in use across WS. **1st row** (RS) Reading row 1 from right to left, rep 6 patt sts to last st, K last st of the chart. **2nd row** Reading row 2 from left to right patt first st, rep 6 patt sts to end. Cont in this way until row 16 of chart has been worked. Rep 5th to 16th rows until back measures 25(28:33:37)cm from cast-on edge, ending with a WS row.
Shape shoulders Cast off 20(22:24:26) sts at beg of next 2 rows. Leave rem 21(23: 25:27) sts on a holder.

FRONT

Work as back until front measures 12 rows less than back to shoulders, ending with a WS row.
Shape neck **Next row** Patt 24(26:28:30) sts, turn. Cont on these sts only for 1st side and leave rem sts on a spare needle. Keeping patt correct, dec one st at neck edge on next 4 rows. 20(22:24:26) sts. Patt 3 rows straight. Cast off. With RS facing, sl centre 13(15:17:19) sts on to a holder, rejoin yarn to rem sts, patt to end. Dec one st at neck edge on next 4 rows. 20(22:24: 26) sts. Patt 7 rows straight. Cast off.

SLEEVES

Using 4mm needles and A, cast on 62(66: 70:74) sts. Work 4 rows g st. Beg with a K row, work 5 rows st st. Change to 3¼mm needles. **Dec row** [P2 tog] to end. 31(33:35:37) sts. **1st rib row** K1, [P1, K1] to end. **2nd rib row** P1,[K1, P1] to end. Rep 1st rib row once. **Inc row** Rib 2(4:3: 3), [inc in next st, rib 4(7:3:5)] to last 4(5:4:4) sts, inc in next st, rib 3(4:3:3). 37(37:43:43) sts. Change to 4mm needles. Cont in patt from the chart, as for back, working rows 1 to 16, then rep rows 5 to 16 throughout and at the same time, inc one st at each end of every 3rd row, taking inc sts into patt, until there are 53(57:61: 65) sts. Patt straight until sleeve measures 16(17:18:19)cm from cast-on edge, ending with a WS row. Cast off loosely.

NECKBAND

Join right shoulder seam. With RS facing, 3¼mm needles and A, K up 11 sts down left front neck, K across 13(15:17:19) sts at centre front, K up 15 sts up right front neck then K across 21(23:25:27) sts of back neck. 60(64:68:72) sts. Beg P row, st st 3 rows. **Picot row** K1, [yo, K2 tog] to last st, K1. Beg with a P row, st st 3 rows. Cast off loosely. Fold neckband to WS at picot row and pin in position. Catch stitch loosley in place and neaten ends.

BUTTONHOLE BAND

With RS facing, 3¼mm needles and B, K up 20(22:24:26) sts evenly across the left front shoulder and 3 sts across edge of neckband. 23(25:27:29) sts. **Next row** P1, [K1, P1] to end. **Next row** Rib 3, [yo, K2 tog, rib 6(7:8:9)] twice, yo, K2 tog, rib 2. Rib 1 row. Cast off in rib.

BUTTON BAND

Work to match buttonhole band omitting buttonholes.

TO MAKE UP

Sew buttons on button band to correspond to buttonholes. Mark position of underarms 12(13:14:15)cm down from shoulders on back and front. Sew on sleeves between the markers. Join side and sleeve seams. Thread the shirring elastic through rib rows above sleeve frills.

HAT

Using 3¼mm needles and A, cast on 85(91) sts. **1st rib row** (RS) K1, [P1, K1] to end. **2nd rib row** P1, [K1, P1] to end. Rep these 2 rows for 3cm, ending **2nd rib row**. Change to 4mm needles. Cont in st st from chart as back. Work 1st to 16th rows.
Shape work Cont in spot patt as on rows 5 to 16, noting that it will not be possible to keep patt in alignment, but try to alternate each row of spots above previous spots. **1st dec row** With B, K5, K2 tog, [K10(11), K2 tog] 6 times, K6. 78 (84) sts. Patt 5 rows. **2nd dec row** With B, K5, K2 tog, [K9(10), K2 tog] 6 times, K5. 71(77) sts. Patt 5 rows. **3rd dec row** With B, K4, K2 tog, [K8(9), K2 tog] 6 times, K5. 64(70) sts. Patt 5 rows. **4th dec row** With B, K4, K2 tog, [K7(8), K2 tog] 6 times, K4. 57(63) sts. Patt 5 rows. **5th dec row** With B, K3, K2tog, [K6(7), K2 tog] 6 times, K4. 50(56) sts. Patt 5 rows. **6th dec row** With B, K3, K2 tog, [K5(6), K2 tog] 6 times, K3. 43(49) sts. Patt 5 rows. **7th dec row** With B, K2, K2 tog, [K4(5), K2 tog] 6 times, K3. 36(42) sts. Patt 5 rows. **8th dec row** With B, K2, K2 tog, [K3(4), K2 tog] 6 times, K2. 29(35) sts. Patt 5 rows. **9th dec row** With B, K1, K2 tog, [K2(3), K2 tog] 6 times, K2. 22(28) sts. Patt 5 rows. **10th dec row** With B, K1, K2 tog, [K1(2), K2 tog] 6 times, K1. 15(21) sts. Patt 5 rows. **11th dec row** With B, [K1, K2 tog] to end. 10(14) sts. Patt 5 rows. **12th dec row** [K2 tog] to end. 5(7) sts. P 1 row. Cut yarn, thread end through rem sts, draw up and secure. Join seam. Make a tassel in C and attach to top.
Loop trim With WS facing, using crochet hook and C, insert hook through first st of 1st rib row, yrh and draw loop through to WS, * insert the hook through next st of 1st rib row, wind yarn round 1st finger of left hand to form a 4cm long loop, yrh after loop on finger and draw yarn through to WS then through

loop on hook (one 4cm long loop has been worked on RS of work.) Rep from * to end of 1st rib row. Fasten off. Work in same way along every alt rib row.

BOOTEES

Using 3¼mm needles and A, cast on 31 (37) sts. **1st rib row** K1, [P1, K1] to end. **2nd rib row** P1, [K1, P1] to end. Rep these 2 rows twice more. Change to 4mm needles. Cont in patt from chart as back. Work rows 1 to 10.

Shape instep **1st row** With B, K22(25), turn. **2nd row** With B, P13, turn. Keeping patt correct, cont on these 13 sts only. Patt 10 rows. **Next row** With B and using needle holding first set of 9(12) sts, K up 9 sts along row-ends of 1st side of instep, K across 13 sts of instep, K up 9 sts along 2nd side of instep then K rem 9(12) sts. 49(55) sts. P 1 row B. Patt rows 13 to 16. Cont in B, st st 2 rows.

Shape foot **1st row** (RS) [K1, K2 tog tbl, K19(22), K2 tog] twice, K1. P 1 row. **2nd row** [K1, K2 tog tbl, K17(20), K2 tog] twice, K1. Cast off rem 41(47) sts. Join foot and leg seams using a flat seam. Work loop trim, as hat, into 5 of the 6 rib rows, but make 3 cm long loops.

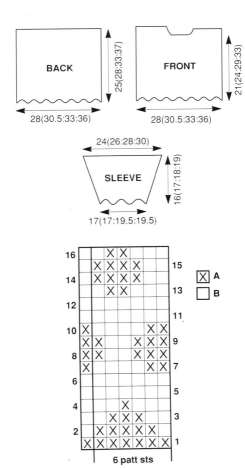

BACK 25(28:33:37) 28(30.5:33:36)

FRONT 21(24:29:33) 28(30.5:33:36)

SLEEVE 24(26:28:30) 16(17:18:19) 17(17:19.5:19.5)

⊠ A
☐ B

6 patt sts

Peruvian Sweater and Hat

A brightly striped sweater and hat decorated with a row of figures worked from a simple chart.

Skill Rating Experienced
Sizes To fit age 3(6:12) months
Sweater: To fit chest 16(18:20)in/41(46:51)cm
Actual size 48(53:58)cm
Length to shoulder 22(25:29)cm *Sleeve seam* 18(20:23)cm
Hat: To fit up to 46cm head
Materials Sweater and Hat 1 x 50g ball of 50% Courtelle/40% Bri-Nylon/10% wool DK in each of red (colour A), royal blue (B), pink (C), yellow (D), cream (E), kingfisher (F), emerald (G) and bottle (H)
We used Wendy Family Choice DK
Pair each 3¼mm and 4mm knitting needles
Tension 24 sts and 32 rows to 10cm over st st on 4mm needles

SWEATER

BACK

Using 3¼mm needles and E, cast on 51(55:61) sts. Break off E and join in A. **1st rib row** (RS) K1, [P1, K1] to end. **2nd rib row** P1, [K1, P1] to end. Rep these 2 rows for 3cm, ending with a RS row. **Next row** Rib 5(3:2), * M1, rib 8(7:8), rep from * to last 6(3:3) sts, M1, rib to end. 57(63:69) sts. Change to 4mm needles.

Commence pattern **1st row** K with D. **2nd row** P [1D, 1C, 4D] to last 3 sts, 1D, 1C, 1D. **3rd row** K 3C, [3D, 3C] to end. **4th row** P[4C, 1D, 1C] to last 3 sts, 3C. **5th row** K with C. **6th row** P with E. **7th row** K with E. **8th row** P with G. **9th row** K with G. **10th row** P with H. **11th row** K with H. **12th row** P with B. Cont in patt from chart, beg at size indicated, reading odd-numbered (K) rows from right to left and even-numbered (P) rows from left to right, stranding yarns not in use loosely across back of work, until 14 chart rows are completed. **27th row** K with B. **28th row** P with F. **29th row** K with F. **30th and 31st rows** As 6th and 7th rows. **32nd-36th rows** As 1st-5th rows but reading P for K and K for P. **37th row** K with A. **38th row** P with A. **39th row** As 37th row. **40th and 41st rows** As 10th and 11th rows. **42nd and 43rd rows** As 8th and 9th rows. **44th row** P with D. **45th row** As 1st row. **46th and 47th rows** As 6th and 7th rows. **48th and 49th rows** As 28th and 29th rows. **50th row** As 12th row. **51st row** As 27th row. **52nd and 53rd rows** As 50th

and 51st rows. **54th and 55th rows** As 10th and 11th rows. **56th row** P with C. Keeping patt correct as follows, at the same time, when 56(64:78) rows in all have been worked, shape neck as given below. **57th row** As 5th row. **58th row** As 38th row. **59th and 60th rows** As 37th and 38th rows. **61st row** As 1st row. **62nd row** As 44th row. **63rd row** As 7th row. **64th row** As 6th row. **65th row** As 29th row. **66th and 67th rows** As 28th and 29th rows. **68th and 69th rows** As 8th and 9th rows. **70th row** As 8th row. **71st row** As 11th row. **72nd row** As 10th row. **73rd-76th rows** Rep 37th and 38th rows twice. **77th row** As 5th row. **78th row** As 56th row. **79th row** As 1st row. **80th row** As 44th row. **81st row** As 7th row. **82nd row** As 6th row. **83rd row** As 27th row. **84th row** As 12th row.

Shape neck **Next row** Patt 19(23:25), turn and leave rem sts on a spare needle. Dec one st at neck edge on next 3(5:5) rows. Cast off rem 16(18:20) sts. With RS facing, slip centre 19(17:19) sts onto a holder, rejoin yarn and patt to end. Complete to match other side of neck.

FRONT

Work as given for back until 46(56:70) rows have been completed.

Shape neck **Next row** Patt 22(24:26), turn and leave rem sts on a spare needle. Dec one st at neck edge on next 6 rows. 16(18:20) sts. Cont without shaping until work matches back to shoulder, ending with a P row. Cast off. With RS facing, sl

centre 13(15:17) sts on to a holder, rejoin yarn and patt to end. Complete to match other side of neck.

SLEEVES

Using 3¼mm needles and E, cast on 33(35:37) sts. Join in A, work 3cm K1, P1 rib as given for back, ending with a RS row. **Next row** Rib 1(2:1), * M1, rib 6(10:5), rep from * to last 2(3:1) sts, M1, rib to end. 39(39:45) sts. Change to 4mm needles. Cont in patt as given for back centering marked st on chart, at the same time, inc one st at each end of the 7th and every foll 6th row, working inc sts into patt until there are 49(53:57) sts. Cont straight until work measures 18(20:23)cm from beg. Cast off.

NECKBAND

Join right shoulder seam. Using 3¼mm needles, A and with RS facing, K up 18 sts down left front neck, K 13(15:17) front neck sts, K up 18 sts up right front neck and 4(6:6) sts down right back neck, K5, M1, K9(7:9), M1, K5 across back neck sts, K up 4(6:6) sts up left back neck. 78(82:86) sts. Work 5 rows, K1, P1 rib. Join in E. Work 1 more row, then cast off loosely in rib.

TO MAKE UP

Join left shoulder and neckband seam. Place markers 10(11:12)cm down from shoulders on back and front. Sew in sleeves between markers. Join side and sleeve seams.

HAT

EAR FLAPS

Make 2 Using 4mm needles and B, cast on 9 sts. **1st row** P to end. Commence patt: beg with a K row cont in st st working patt from chart, centering marked st as indicated, at the same time, inc one st at each end of 2nd and every foll alt row, working motif over 13 sts then inc sts at each side in B. Cont until 14 rows of chart are completed. 23 sts. Leave sts on a holder.

HAT

Using 4mm needles and B, cast on 11 sts, with RS facing, K across sts of 1st ear flap, cast on 21 sts, with RS facing, K across sts of 2nd ear flap, cast on 11 sts. 89 sts. Beg with row 28, cont in patt as for back of sweater until row 52 has been completed.

Shape crown Keeping patt correct: **1st row** K2, [K3, K2 tog] to last 2 sts, K2. 72

sts. Patt 5 rows straight. **7th row** K2, [K2, K2 tog] to last 2 sts, K2. 55 sts. Patt 5 rows straight. **13th row** K2, [K2 tog] to last 3 sts, K3. 30 sts. Patt 1 row straight. Cont in F only. **15th row** * K5, sl 1, K1, psso, K1, K2 tog, K5, rep from * once. 26 sts. **16th and every foll alt row** P to end. **17th row** * K4, sl 1, K1, psso, K1, K2 tog, K4, rep from * once. 22 sts. **19th row** * K3, sl 1, K1, psso, K1, K2 tog, K3, rep from * once. 18 sts. **21st row** * K2, sl 1, K1, psso, K1, K2 tog, K2, rep from * once. 14 sts. **23rd row** * K1, sl 1, K1, psso, K1, K2 tog, K1, rep from * once. 10 sts. **25th row** * Sl 1, K1, psso, K1, K2 tog, rep from * once. 6 sts. Break off yarn, thread through sts, pull tight and fasten off. Using 3¼mm needles, A and with RS facing, K up 125 sts along lower edge. K 1 row. Join in E, K 1 row, cast off. Join back seam. Sew on small tassel.

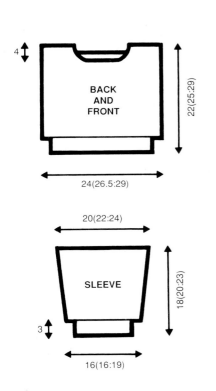

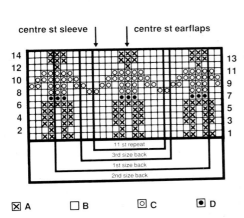

Dungaree Outfit

This adorable matching set is child's play to knit and it's just perfect for keeping baby snug.

Skill Rating Easy

Sizes To fit up to age 3(6:12) months

To fit chest 41(46:51)cm/16(18:20)in *To fit height* 60(70:80)cm

Sweater: Actual size chest 41(49:55)cm

Length to shoulder 18(21:24)cm *Sleeve seam* 13.5(15:16.5)cm

Dungarees: Actual size chest 41(50:63)cm

Hips 63(75:89)cm *Length* 46(52:64)cm

Materials Sweater 2(2:3) x 50g balls of 55% wool/25% acrylic/20% nylon DK in yellow (colour A)

Dungarees 3(4:5) balls same in green (B)

Hat and Socks One ball same each of A and B

We used Patons Diploma Gold DK

Pair each of 3¼mm and 4mm knitting needles • Cable needle
2 small buttons for sweater • 4 small buttons for dungarees

Tension 20 sts and 40 rows to 10cm over g st, 22 sts and 30 rows to 10cm over st st, on 4mm needles

Special Abbreviations

CD8B = slip next 4 sts onto cable needle, hold at back, K next st tog with 1st st on cable needle, rep until all sts are worked, making 4 sts from 8

CD8F = as CD8B but holding cable needle in front

SWEATER

The sweater is worked sideways from cuff to cuff. Using 3¼mm needles and A, cast on 26(32:38) sts. K 8 rows. Change to 4mm needles. Cont in g st, inc one st at each end of 9th and every foll 8th row until there are 36(42:48) sts. K 5(11:17) rows.

Shape for back and front Cast on 18(21:24) sts at beg of next 2 rows. 72(84: 96) sts. K 20(24:28) rows.

Shape neck **Next row** (RS) K36(42:48) sts, turn and complete back neck on these sts. Dec one st at neck edge on next and foll alt row. 34(40:46) sts. K 15(19:21) rows.

Back opening **Next row** (WS) Cast off 8 sts, K to end. **Next row** (RS) K 26(32:38) sts. **Next row** (WS) Cast on 8 sts, K all 34(40:46) sts. K 14(18:20) rows. Inc one st at neck edge on next and foll alt row. 36(42:48) sts. Leave sts on a holder.

Shape front neck With RS facing, rejoin yarn at neck edge to 36(42:48) sts on spare needle, cast off 3 sts, K to end. Dec one st at neck edge on next and foll 1(2:3) alt rows. 31(36:41) sts. K 32(36:36) rows. Inc one st at neck edge on next and foll 1(2:3) alt rows.

Join for right shoulder **Next row** (WS) K33(39:45) sts of front, cast on 3 sts, K36(42:48) sts from holder. 72(84:96) sts. K 20(24:28) rows.

Shape sides Cast off 18(21:24) sts at beg of next 2 rows. 36(42:48) sts.

Right sleeve K5(11:17) rows. Dec one st at each end of next and every foll 8th row until 26(32:38) sts rem. K 8 rows. Change to 3¼mm needles. K 8 rows. Cast off.

Neckband Using 3¼mm needles, A and with RS facing, K up 12(14:16) sts across left back neck, 30(34:38) sts around front neck and 12(14:16) sts across right back neck. 54(62:70) sts. K 6 rows. Cast off.

TO MAKE UP

Join side and sleeve seams. Make 2 button loops at neck opening. Sew on buttons.

DUNGAREES

LEGS

Left leg Using 3¼mm needles and B, cast on 40(48:56) sts. K 8 rows. Change to 4mm needles.

Make ankle pleats **Next row** (RS) K4(6: 8), * [cast on 4 sts, K6] twice, cast on 4 sts *, K8(12:16), rep from * to *, K4(6:8). 64 (72:80) sts. Beg P, st st 3 rows. Inc one st at each end of next and every foll 3rd row until there are 82(98:118) sts. Work 1 row.

Shape crotch **1st row** (RS) Cast off 1(2:4) sts, K to end. **2nd row** (WS) Cast off 3(5:7) sts, P to end. Dec one st at each end of next 3 rows, then at end only of next and foll alt row. 70(83:99) sts. Work 1 row.

Right leg Work to match left leg, reversing shapings.

BODY

With WS facing, P across 69(82:98) sts of right leg, P last st of right leg tog with 1st st of left leg, P rem sts of left leg. 139(165: 197) sts. Work straight until dungarees measure 34(39:48)cm from cast-on edge, ending P row.

Make waist pleats **Next row** (RS) K6(8: 10), * [CD8F, K1(2:3)] 3 times, K6(10:16), [CD8B, K1(2:3)] 3 times *, K9(11:15), rep from * to *, K4(6:8). 91(117:149) sts. Change to 3¼mm needles. K8 rows.

Make straps and bib **Next row** (WS) Cast off 4(7:11) sts, K8 and leave 9 sts on a holder for strap, cast off 18(26:34) sts, K28(32:40) more sts, cast off 18(26:34) sts, K8 and leave 9 sts on a holder for strap, cast off rem sts.

Make bib With RS facing, rejoin yarn to centre 29(33:41) sts. K 20(30:40) rows.

Make buttonholes **Next row** (RS) K3, yo, [K2 tog] twice, yo, K to last 7 sts, yo, [K2 tog] twice, yo, K3. K 4 rows. Cast off.

Make straps With RS facing, rejoin yarn, K until strap measures 18(20:24)cm. Cast off.

TO MAKE UP

Press st st lightly. Press waist pleats into shape. Fold ankle pleats to match, press fold in each pleat and catch stitch down. Join back and crotch seams. Join inside leg seams. Sew buttons onto straps.

HAT

Using 3¼mm needles and B, cast on 66(82:98) sts. K8 rows. Change to 4mm needles.

Make pleats **Next row** (RS) K3(5:7), * [cast on 4 sts, K6] twice, cast on 4 sts **, K4(8:12) ***, rep from * to *** twice, then from * to ** once, K3(5:7). 114(130:146) sts. Beg P, st st 19(23:27) rows.

Shape crown **1st row** (RS) K1, [K2 tog, K10(12:14), skpo] 8 times, K1. 98(114: 130) sts. **2nd and every WS row** P. **3rd row** (RS) K1, [K2 tog, K 8(10:12), skpo] 8 times, K1. 82(98:114) sts. Cont to dec in this way on every RS row until 34 sts rem. P 1 row. **Next row** (RS) K1, [K2 tog, skpo] 8 times, K1. 18 sts. P 1 row. **Next row** K1, [K2 tog] 8 times, K1. 10 sts. Break yarn, thread through sts, draw up and secure.

TO MAKE UP

Sew back seam. Press lightly. Make pom-pom with A and sew to the top of the hat.

SOCKS

Right sock Using 3¼mm needles and A, cast on 28(32:36) sts. K 8 rows. Change to 4mm needles. Beg K, st st 14(16:18) rows.

Divide for heel **1st row** (RS) K12(14: 16) sts, sl them onto a holder, K to end.

Using spare needle and contrast yarn, cast on 12(14:16) sts. **2nd row** (WS) P16(18: 20) sts of sock, then 12(14:16) cast-on sts. 28(32:36)sts. St-st 16(22:28) rows.

Shape toe Change to 3¼mm needles. **1st row** (RS) K1, [K2 tog, K9(11:13), skpo] twice, K1. 24(28:32) sts. **2nd and every alt row** K. **3rd row** K1, [K2 tog, K7(9:11), skpo] twice, K1. 20(24:28) sts. Cont to dec in this way on every RS row until 12(16: 20) sts rem. Cast off.

Shape heel With 3¼mm needles and

RS facing, K 12(14:16) sts from holder, undo contrast yarn cast-on sts and K up 12(14: 16) sts from loops. 24(28:32) sts. **1st and every WS row** K. **2nd row** (RS) K1, [K2 tog, K7(9:11), skpo] twice, K1. Cont to dec in this way until 8(12:16) sts rem. Cast off.

Left sock Work to match right sock reversing shapings.

To make up Sew heel seams. Join toe and side seams. Using B, make 2 pompoms and sew one onto each sock.

Cricket Cardigan

This pure cotton V-neck cardigan is worked in a simple cable stitch pattern.

Skill Rating Medium
Sizes To fit age 6(12) months
To fit chest 18(20)in/46(51)cm
Actual size 50(60)cm
Length to shoulder 28(33)cm *Sleeve seam* 16(19)cm
Materials 3(4) x 50g balls of 100% cotton DK in white (colour A)
and 1 ball same in yellow (B)
We used Hayfield Raw Cotton DK
Pair each 3mm and 4mm knitting needles
Cable needle • 4 buttons
Tension 24 sts and 28 rows to 10cm over patt on 4mm needles
Special Abbreviations
C3R = slip next 2 sts onto cable needle, hold at back of work, K1,
then K2 from cable needle
C3L = slip next st onto cable needle, hold at front of work, K2,
then K1 from cable needle

BACK

Using 3mm needles and A, cast on 61(73) sts. **1st rib row** With B, K1, [P1, K1] to end. **2nd rib row** With B, P1, [K1, P1] to end. With A, rep these 2 rows twice. With B rep these 2 rows once. With A rep these 2 rows once. Change to 4mm needles and cont in A only. **Next row** (RS) [K1, P1, K3, P1] to last st, K1. **Next row** [P1, K1, P3, K1] to last st, P1.

Commence pattern **1st row** (RS) [K1, P1, C3R, P1, K1, P1, C3L, P1] to last st, K1. **2nd row** [P1, K1, P3, K1] to last st, P1. **3rd row** [K1, P1, K3, P1] to last st, P1. **4th row** As 2nd row. These 4 rows form patt. Cont in patt until work measures 28(33)cm from beg, ending with a WS row. Cast off.

LEFT FRONT

Using 3mm needles and A, cast on 26(32) sts. Work K1, P1 rib in stripe patt as given for back. Change to 4mm needles and cont in A only. **Next row** [K1, P1, K3, P1] to last 2 sts, K1, P1. **Next row** K1, P1, [K1, P3, K1, P1] to end.

Commence pattern **1st row** (RS) [K1, P1, C3R, P1, K1, P1, C3L, P1] to last 2(8) sts, K1, P1, *2nd size only* C3R, P1, K1, P1. **2nd row** [K1, P1, K1, P3] to last 2 sts, K1, P1. **3rd row** [K1, P1, K3, P1] to last 2 sts, K1, P1. **4th row** As 2nd row. These 4 rows form patt. Cont in patt until work measures 15(18)cm from beg, ending with a WS row. (For right front, ending with a RS row.)

Shape front edge Cont in patt as set, dec one st at end of next and every foll 4th row until 20(24) sts rem. Cont without shaping until work measures same as back to shoulder, ending with a WS row. Cast off loosely in patt.

RIGHT FRONT

Using 3mm needles and A, cast on 26(32) sts. Beg rib P1, work in stripe patt as given for back. Change to 4mm needles. **Next row** P1, [K1, P1, K3, P1] to last st, K1. **Next row** P1, [K1, P3, K1, P1] to last st, K1.

Commence pattern **1st row** (RS) *2nd size only* P1, K1, P1, C3L, *both sizes* [P1, K1, P1, C3R, P1, K1, P1, C3L] to last 2 sts, P1, K1. **2nd row** P1, [K1, P3, K1, P1] to last st, K1. **3rd row** [P1, K1, P1, K3] to last 2 sts, P1, K1. **4th row** As 2nd row. These 4 rows form patt. Complete to match left front.

SLEEVES

Using 3mm needles and A, cast on 37(37) sts. Change to B, work 10 rows K1, P1 rib in stripe patt as given for back. Change to 4mm needles. Cont in A only. **Next row** [K1, P1, K3, P1] to last st, K1. **Next row** [P1, K1, P3, K1] to last st, P1. Work in patt as given for back, inc one st at each end of 3rd and every foll alt row until there are 61(69) sts, working inc sts into patt. Cont without shaping until work measures 16(19)cm from beg, ending with a WS row. Cast off.

FRONT BAND

Join shoulder seams, matching patt. Using 3mm needles, A and with RS facing, beg at cast on edge K up 73(89) sts up right front, 21(23) sts from back neck and 73(89) sts down left front. 167(201) sts. **Next row** (WS) P1, [K1, P1] to end. **Next row** Using B, K1, [P1, K1] to end. Cont in rib, using B work 1 row, using A work 1 row. **Buttonhole row** Rib 3, [cast off 3, rib 10] 3 times, cast off 3, rib to end. **Next row** Rib as set, casting on 3 sts over cast off sts of previous row. Work 1 more row. Using B work 2 rows, using A work 2 rows. Cast off.

TO MAKE UP

Press according to directions on the ball band. Place markers 12.5(14.5)cm down from shoulders on back and fronts for armholes. Sew in sleeves between markers. Join side and sleeve seams. Sew on buttons.

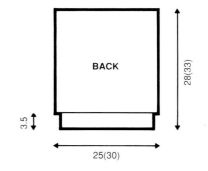

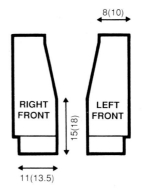

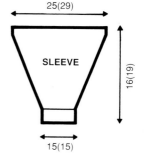

Frilled Top and Trousers

A bright and zany cotton two piece with a moss stitch gathered peplum, combining Fair Isle and intarsia techniques.

Skill Rating Experienced
Sizes To fit age 6(9:12:18) months
Top: To fit chest 18(19:20:21)in/46(48:51:54)cm
Actual size 52(56:59:62)cm
Length to shoulder 25(27:27:28)cm *Sleeve seam* 15(17:18.5:20)cm
Trousers: Length 37(40:43:45)cm
Materials Top and Trousers 5 x 50g balls of 100% cotton DK
in blue (colour A), 2 balls same in pink (B) and 1 ball same in each of
yellow (C), white (D), red (E), and green (F)
We used Hayfield Raw Cotton DK
Pair each of 3¼mm and 4mm knitting needles
2 small buttons • Waist length of narrow elastic
Tension 24 sts and 27 rows to 10cm over patt on 4mm needles

TOP

BACK

Using 4mm needles and B, cast on 130 (138:146:154) sts. **1st row** (RS) [K1, P1] to end. **2nd row** [P1, K1] to end. Rep these 2 rows for 3cm, ending with a 1st row. **Dec row** [P2 tog] to end. 65(69:73:77) sts. Beg with a K row, cont in st st and patt from chart 1. Read odd numbered (K) rows from right to left and even numbered (P) rows from left to right. Strand colours not in use loosely across WS of work. Patt rows 1 to 26(32:32:36). Patt rows 37 to 44. Working from chart 2, use a separate ball of yarn for each area of colour and twist yarns tog on WS of work when changing colour to avoid a hole. **1st row** (RS) K2(4: 2:4) D, * patt 13(13:15:15) sts of row 1, K3 D, rep from * 3 times, ending last rep K2 (4:2:4)D. With sts as set, patt rows 2 to 14 of chart 2. Patt rows 1 to 8 of chart 3, stranding yarn not in use loosely across back of work. Cont in B. **1st rib row** (RS) K1, [P1, K1] to end. **2nd rib row** P1, [K1, P1] to end. Rep these 2 rows once. Cast off loosely in rib.

FRONT

Work as given for back.

SLEEVES

Using 3¼mm needles and B, cast on 27 (29:33:35) sts. Rib 9 rows as at top of back.

Inc row Rib 2(0:2:3), [inc in next st, rib 2(3:3:2)] 7(7:7:9) times, inc in next st, rib 3(0:2:4). 35(37:41:45) sts. Change to 4mm needles. Inc one st at each end of 5th row and every foll 3rd row until there are 53 (59:65:71) sts, at the same time patt from chart 1 working rows 1 to 26, then rows 7 to 12(17:22:27). Cast off loosely with A.

TO MAKE UP

Join cast-off edges of back and front for 12(13:14:15) sts from each side edge. Insert markers 11(12:13.5:15)cm down from shoulders on back and front. Sew in sleeves between markers. Join side and sleeve seams. Sew buttons to rib at top of back, on the 17th(18th:19th:20th) st from each side edge. With B, embroider button loops at top of front rib to correspond to buttons.

TROUSERS

BACK

First leg Using 3¼mm needles and A, cast on 29(29:35:35) sts. Rib 2 rows as at end of top back. Change to 4mm needles. Cont from chart 1, rep rows 7 to 26 for patt throughout, working 1st and 2nd sizes as marked for 4th size of back and working 3rd and 4th sizes as marked for 1st size of sleeves. Inc one st at end of 5th row and every foll 8th row, taking inc sts into patt, until there are 34(36:40:42) sts. Patt straight until work measures

18(20: 22:24)cm from beg, ending with a P row.
Shape crotch Dec one st at shaped edge on next 4(3:4:3) rows, ending with K row. Cut off yarns. Leave rem 30(33:36:39) sts on a spare needle.
Second leg Work as given for first left, but inc at beg not end of rows. **Joining row** Patt across sts of 2nd leg to last st, P tog last st of 2nd leg and first st of 1st leg, patt across rem sts of 1st leg. 59(65:71:77) sts. Patt straight until work measures 15(16: 17:18)cm from joining row. Change to 3¼mm needles. Cont in A. Rib 3 rows. **Eyelet row** [Rib 3, yrn, rib 2 tog] to last 4(5:1: 2) sts, rib to end. Rib 3 rows. Cast off in rib.

FRONT

Work as given for back.

TO MAKE UP

Join crotch shaping on back and on front. Join inner leg seams. Join side seams. Thread elastic through eyelet row, adjust to fit and secure ends.

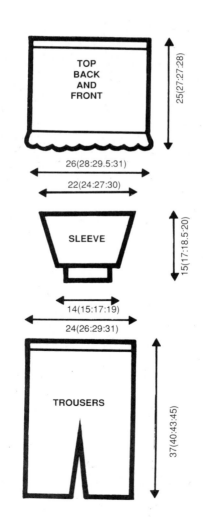

CHART 1

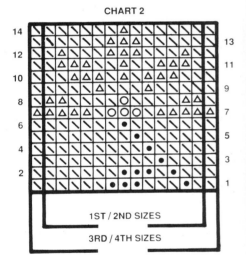

REPEAT 24 STS
3RD SIZE BACK
4TH SIZE BACK
1ST SIZE SLEEVE
2ND SIZE SLEEVE
1ST SIZE BACK / 3RD SIZE SLEEVE
2ND SIZE BACK / 4TH SIZE SLEEVE

CHART 2

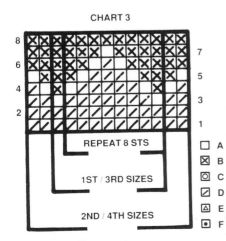

1ST / 2ND SIZES

3RD / 4TH SIZES

CHART 3

REPEAT 8 STS

1ST / 3RD SIZES

2ND / 4TH SIZES

☐	A
☒	B
◉	C
◹	D
△	E
⊡	F

Baby Layette

Traditional baby clothes knitted in a simple lace and garter stitch pattern. The dress can be made in two lengths.

Skill Rating Experienced
Sizes To fit age 0-6 months
Shawl: 122cm square approx *Dress: To fit chest* 18in/46cm
Actual size 46cm *Sleeve seam* 17cm
Long dress: Length 75cm *Short dress: Length* 45cm
Materials Shawl 14 x 25g balls of
60% acrylic/40% nylon 2 ply in white
Long dress 7 balls same *Short dress* 5 balls same
Bonnet 1 ball same *Bootees* 1 ball same
We used Patons Fairytale 2 ply
Pair each 2¼mm and 4½mm knitting needles
3½mm crochet hook • 4 small buttons for dress • 1 small button for bonnet
60cm narrow ribbon for bootees
Tension 38 sts and 46 rows to 10cm over st st on 2¼mm needles
20 sts and 48 rows to 10cm over diamond patt on 4½mm needles

SHAWL

Using 4½mm needles cast on 229 sts. Work in diamond pattern. **1st and every alt row** (WS) K. **2nd row** [K6, yfwd, K2 tog tbl, K4] to last st, K1. **4th row** [K4, K2 tog, yfwd, K1, yfwd, K2 tog tbl, K3] to last st, K1. **6th row** [K3, K2 tog, yfwd, K3, yfwd, K2 tog tbl, K2] to last st, K1. **8th row** [K2, K2 tog, yfwd, K5, yfwd, K2 tog tbl, K1] to last st, K1. **10th row** [K1, K2 tog, yfwd, K7, yfwd, K2 tog tbl] to last st, K1. **12th row** K2 tog, yfwd, [K9, yfwd, sl 1, K2 tog, psso, yfwd] to last 11 sts, K9, yfwd, K2 tog tbl. **14th row** K12, [yfwd, K2 tog tbl, K10] to last st, K1. **16th row** [K1, yfwd, K2 tog tbl, K7, K2 tog, yfwd] to last st, K1. **18th row** [K2, yfwd, K2 tog tbl, K5, K2 tog, yfwd, K1] to last st, K1. **20th row** [K3, yfwd, K2 tog tbl, K3, K2 tog, yfwd, K2] to last st, K1. **22nd row** [K4, yfwd, K2 tog tbl, K1, K2 tog, yfwd, K3] to last st, K1. **24th row** [K5, yfwd, sl 1, K2 tog, psso, yfwd, K4] to last st, K1. These 24 rows form diamond patt. Rep last 24 rows until length equals width (approx), ending with a 24th row of patt. Cast off loosely knitwise. Block shawl by pinning out around edges and press very lightly foll directions on ball band, taking care not to flatten patt.

EDGING

Using 4½mm needles cast on 6 sts. K1 row. **1st row** (RS) K2, yfwd, K2 tog, yfwd, K2. **2nd row** K2, [yfwd, K1] twice, yfwd, K2 tog, K1. **3rd row** K2, yfwd, K2 tog, yfwd, K3, yfwd, K2. **4th row** K2, yfwd, K5, yfwd, K1, yfwd, K2 tog, K1. **5th row** K2, yfwd, K2 tog, yfwd, K2 tog tbl, K3, K2 tog, yfwd, K2. **6th row** K3, yfwd, K2 tog tbl, K1, K2 tog, yfwd, K2, yfwd, K2 tog, K1. **7th row** K2, yfwd, K2 tog, K2, yfwd, sl 1, K2 tog, psso, yfwd, K4. **8th row** Cast off 7 sts, K2, yfwd, K2 tog, K1. 6 sts. These 8 rows form edging patt. Rep 8 rows until edging, when slightly stretched, fits around shawl edges, easing edging round corners and ending with an 8th row of patt. Cast off.

TO MAKE UP

Join cast-on and cast-off ends of edging. Sew in position around shawl. Pin out edging and press very lightly foll directions on ball band.

LONG DRESS

Note: Both dresses are identical except for length of skirt.

BACK

Using 4½mm needles cast on 109 sts. Rep 24 row diamond patt as given for shawl 10 times in all, place coloured marker at centre of last row. Change to 2¼mm needles. **Next row** (WS) P3, [P2 tog, P3] 20 times, P2 tog, P4. 88 sts. Beg K row, cont in st st until back measures 2cm from marker, ending with a P row.
Shape armholes Cast off 3 sts at beg of next 2 rows. Dec one st at each end of next 3 rows. P1 row. Dec one st at each end of next and foll 2 alt rows. 70 sts **. Cont in st st until back measures 11cm from marker, ending with a P row.
Shape shoulders Cast off 6 sts at beg of next 6 rows. Leave rem 34 sts on a holder.

FRONT

Work as back to **. Cont in st st until front measures 7cm from marker, ending with a P row.
Shape neck **Next row** K24, K2 tog, turn. Cont on these sts only and leave rem sts on a spare needle. Dec one st at neck edge on next 7 rows. 18 sts. Cont straight until front matches back to shoulder, ending at armhole edge.
Shape shoulder Cast off 6 sts at beg of next and foll alt row. Work 1 row. Cast off rem 6 sts. With RS facing, sl centre 18 sts onto a holder, rejoin yarn to rem sts, K2 tog, K to end. Complete to match other side.

SLEEVES

Using 2¼mm needles cast on 48 sts. **1st and every rib row** [K1, P1] to end. Rep this row for 2cm, ending with a RS row. **Next row** Rib 24 sts, M1, rib to end. 49 sts. Change to 4½mm needles. Work diamond patt as given for shawl until sleeve measures 17cm, ending with a WS row.
Shape top Cont in patt, cast off 3 sts at beg of next 2 rows. Dec one st at each end of next and every foll alt row until there are 27 sts. **Next row** [P3 tog] 9 times. Cast off rem 9 sts.

NECKBAND

Join right shoulder seam. Using 2¼mm needles and with RS facing, K up 24 sts down left front neck, K across 18 sts of centre front, K up 24 sts up right front neck then K across 34 sts of back neck. 100 sts. Work 3 rows K1, P1 rib. **Next row** K1, [yfwd, K2 tog] to last st, P1. Work 2 more rows K1, P1 rib. Cast off loosely in rib. Fold neckband at row of holes to WS and sew loosely in place.

Join left shoulder for 1cm from armhole edge. With crochet hook, work 1 row DC around shoulder opening. Work another row, making button loops evenly on front shoulder by working [2CH, miss 1DC] 4 times.

LOWER EDGING

Work as for shawl edging to fit around hem.

TO MAKE UP

Block each piece by pinning around edges and pressing foll directions on ball band. Join side and sleeve seams. Sew in sleeves gathering fullness at top. Join and sew on lower edging. Sew on buttons.

SHORT DRESS

Work as for long dress but rep diamond patt until the 24 rows have been worked 5 times in all.

BONNET

Using 2¼mm needles cast on 110 sts. Work 5 rows g st. **Next row** K6, [K2 tog] 49 times, K6. 61 sts. Change to 4½mm needles. Rep 24 row diamond patt as given for shawl, twice. Change to 2¼mm needles. **Next row** K2, [M1, K2] 29 times, K1. 90 sts.

Shape crown Cont in g st. K 6 rows. **Next row** [K5, sl 1, K2 tog, psso, K3] to last 2 sts, K2. 74 sts. K4 rows. **Next row** [K4, sl 1, K2 tog, psso, K2] to last 2 sts, K2. 58 sts. K4 rows. **Next row** [K3, sl 1, K2 tog, psso, K1] to last 2 sts, K2. 42 sts. K4 rows. **Next row** K2, [sl 1, K2 tog, psso, K2] to end. 26 sts. K4 rows. **Next row** K1, [sl 1, K2 tog, psso, K1] to last st, K1. 14 sts. Thread end of yarn through rem sts, draw up and secure.

EDGING

With RS facing join yarn to beg of cast on edge. With crochet hook work 1DC in 1st st, [1DC in next st, 3CH, SS in base of DC, miss next st, 1DC in next st] to end, 1DC into last st. Fasten off.

TO MAKE UP

Do not press. Join crown seam.
Make strap Using 2¼mm needles cast on 4 sts. Work in g-st until strap, when slightly stretched, measures 7cm. **Buttonhole row** K2, yfwd, K2 tog. K4 rows. Cast off. Sew cast-on edge of strap to right front lower edge of bonnet. Sew button to left front lower edge of bonnet.

BOOTEES

Using 2¼mm needles cast on 42 sts. **1st and 2nd rows** K. **3rd row** K1, [yfwd, K2 tog] 20 times, K1. **4th and 5th rows** K. **6th row** P.
Divide for instep **Next row** K28, turn. **Next row** K14, turn. Cont on these 14 sts. K18 rows. With RS facing, and using right needle with 14 sts already on it, K up 14 sts from right side of instep, K14 sts of instep then K up 14 sts down left side of instep, K14 sts on left needle. 70 sts. K3 rows. Beg K row, work 8 rows st st. K4 rows.

Shape foot **1st row** [K1, K2 tog tbl, K29, K2 tog, K1] twice. **2nd and every alt row** K. **3rd row** [K1, K2 tog tbl, K27, K2 tog, K1] twice. **5th row** [K1, K2 tog tbl, K25, K2 tog, K1] twice. **7th row** [K1, K2 tog tbl, K23, K2 tog, K1] twice. 54 sts. **8th row** K. Cast off loosely.

EDGING

Using 4½mm needles, work as given for shawl edging until, when slightly stretched, edging will fit across ankle edge of bootee. Cast off.

TO MAKE UP

Pin out edging and press very lightly foll directions on ball band. Sew to ankle edge. Join cast-on and cast-off edges of edging then join bootee seam. Thread 30cm ribbon through row of holes at each ankle to tie at centre front.

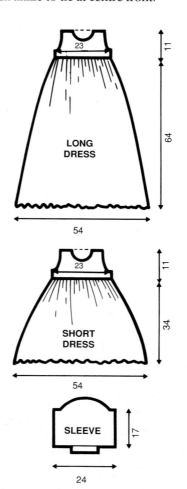

classic
KNITS

Snowflake Pattern Sweater and Beret

This outdoor sweater and beret are knitted in a two-colour snowflake pattern with contrasting borders.

Skill Rating Medium
Sizes To fit age 2-4(6-8) years
To fit chest 22-24(26-28)in/56-61(66-71)cm
Actual size 81(91)cm
Length to shoulder 37(42)cm *Sleeve seam* 25.5(30.5)cm
Materials 5(6) x 50g balls of 55% wool/25% acrylic/20% nylon DK
in cream (colour A), 1 ball same in navy (B) and 3 balls same in red (C)
We used Patons Diploma Gold DK
Pair each of 3¼mm and 4mm knitting needles
Tension 24 sts and 24 rows to 10cm over Fair Isle on
4mm needles
Special Abbreviations
M1K = pick up strand between needles and K it through back of loop
M1P = pick up strand between needles and P it through back of loop

SWEATER

BACK

Using 3¼mm needles and A, cast on 89(99) sts. Change to 4mm needles. Beg and ending with a K row, st st 11 rows. **Next row** (WS) K to mark hemline. **Inc row** K6(5), [M1K, K11(10)] 7(9) times, M1K, K6(4). 97(109) sts. Cont in patt from chart 1, reading odd-numbered P rows from left to right and even-numbered K rows from right to left. Strand colour not in use loosely across WS. Complete 11 rows of chart 1. Cont in patt from chart 2, reading odd-numbered K rows from right to left and even-numbered P rows from left to right **. Work 30 rows of chart 2 twice, then work 1st to 15th(27th) rows again.
Shape neck **Next row** (WS) Patt 38(43) sts, turn. Cont on these sts only for 1st side and leave rem sts on a spare needle. Keeping patt correct, cast off 8 sts at beg of next row. Patt 1 row. Cast off rem 30(35) sts. With WS of work facing, rejoin yarn to inner end of sts on spare needle, cast off 21(23) sts, patt to end. 38(43)sts. Patt 1 row. Keeping patt correct, cast off 8 sts at beg of next row. Cast off rem 30(35)sts.

FRONT

Work as back to **. Work 30 rows of chart 2 twice, then work 1st to 6th(16th) rows again.
Shape neck **Next row** Patt 38(43) sts, turn. Cont on these sts only for 1st side and leave rem sts on a spare needle. Cast off 3 sts at beg of next row. Patt 1 row. Dec one st at neck edge on next 5 rows. 30(35) sts. Patt straight until front matches back to shoulder. Cast off. With RS of work facing, return to sts on spare needle, cast off 21(23) sts, patt to end. Patt 1 row. Complete to match 1st side.

SLEEVES

Using 3¼mm needles and A, cast on 39(43) sts. **1st rib row** (RS) K1, [P1, K1] to end. **2nd rib row** P1, [K1, P1] to end. Rep these 2 rows for 5cm, ending with a 2nd rib row. **Inc row** Rib 2, [M1K, rib 4(8)] 9(5) times, M1K, rib 1. 49 sts. Change to 4mm needles. Reading chart 1 as given for back, patt 11 rows, at the same time, inc one st at each end of 2nd, 5th, 8th and 11th rows. 57 sts. Reading chart 2 as given for back, inc one st at each end of every 3rd row, taking inc sts into patt, until there are 79(87) sts. Patt straight until 37(49) rows are worked

from chart 2, thus ending with 7th(19th) row of chart. Cast off loosely.

COLLAR

Join right shoulder seam. With RS facing, 3¼mm needles and C, K up 13(15) sts down left front neck, 21(23) sts across cast-off sts at centre front, 13(15) sts up right front neck, 8 sts down right back neck, 21(23) sts across cast-off sts at centre back and 8 sts up left back neck. 84(92) sts. P 1 row B. K 1 row A. With A, work 7(8)cm in K1, P1 rib. Cast off loosely in rib.

TO MAKE UP

Join left shoulder and collar seam. Place markers 16.5(18)cm down from shoulders on back and front. Sew in sleeves between markers. Join side and sleeve seams. Fold lower edge of back and front on to WS at hemline and catch loosely in place.

BERET

Using 3¼mm needles and A, cast on 13 sts. Change to 4mm needles. Work in st st, beg with a K row. Work 2 rows. **3rd row** K1, [M1K, K1] to end. 25 sts. Work 4 rows straight. **8th row** P1, [M1P, P1] to end. 49 sts. Work 4 rows straight. **13th row** K1, [M1K, K2] to end. 73 sts. Work 6 rows straight. **20th row** P1, [M1P, P2] to end. 109 sts. Work 6 rows straight. **27th row** K1, [M1K, K3] to end. 145 sts. Work 11 rows straight. **39th row** K1, [K2 tog, K4] to end. 121 sts. Patt 11 rows of chart 1, as given at beg of back. **51st row** As 39th row. 101 sts. Rib 3cm as at beg of sleeve. Cast off in rib. Run a gathering thread through cast-on edge, draw up tightly then join centre back seam. Make a pompom with A and sew to centre top.

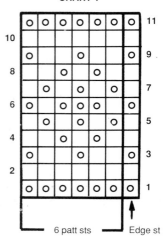

CHART 1

6 patt sts — Edge st

CHART 2

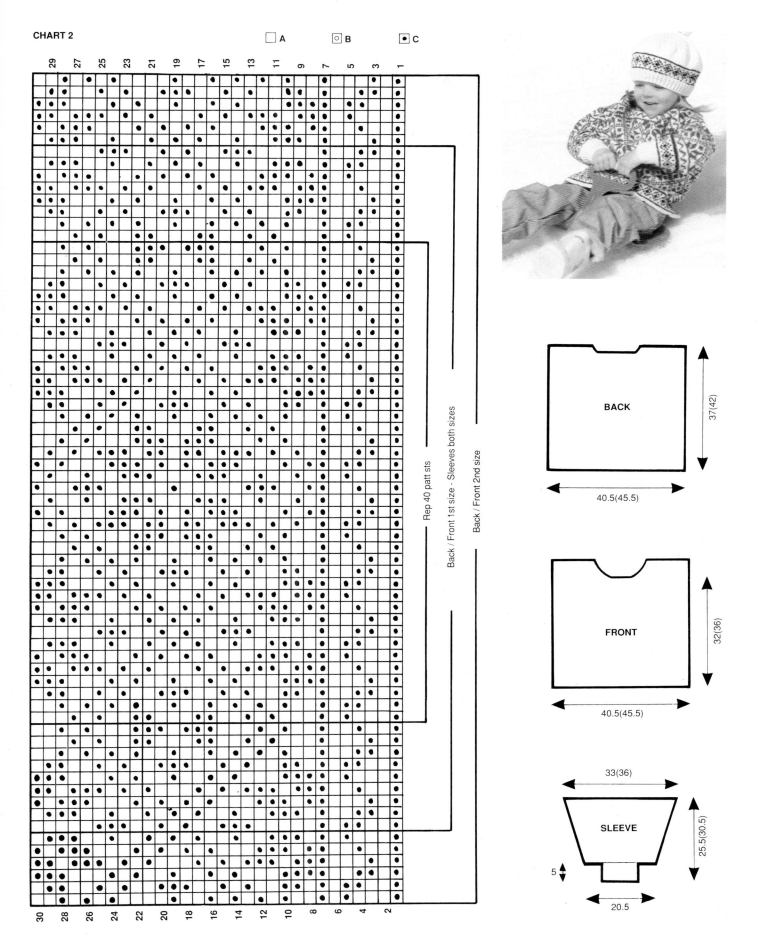

☐ A   ◉ B   ● C

Rep 40 patt sts

Back / Front 1st size - Sleeves both sizes

Back / Front 2nd size

BACK

37(42)

40.5(45.5)

FRONT

32(36)

40.5(45.5)

33(36)

SLEEVE

25.5(30.5)

5

20.5

Cable Dress and Leg Warmers

Knit two shades of DK yarn together to make this quick and easy cabled dress with matching leg warmers.

Skill Rating Medium
Sizes To fit age 2(4:6:8) years
Dress: To fit chest 22(24:26:28)in/56(61:66:71)cm
Actual Size 70(76:82:88)cm
Length to shoulder 55(61:67:73)cm *Sleeve seam* 29(32:35:38)cm
Leg Warmers: Length 27(30:34:38)cm
Materials 3(4:4:4) x 100g balls of 100% acrylic DK in red (colour A)
and 3(4:4:4) balls same in white (B)
We used Littlewoods Economy DK
Pair each of 5mm and 5½mm knitting needles • Cable needle
Tension 19 sts and 21 rows to 10cm over patt on 5½mm needles
Special Abbreviation
C6F = sl next 3 sts on to cable needle and hold at front,
K3 then K3 from cable needle

DRESS

BACK

Using 5mm needles and 1 strand of A and 1 strand of B tog, cast on 53(59:65:71) sts. **1st rib row** (RS) K1, [P1, K1] to end. **2nd rib row** P1, [K1, P1] to end. Rep these 2 rows 4 times, then work 1st rib row again. **Inc row** Rib 2(5:2:5), [inc in next st, rib 3(3:4:4)] 12 times, inc in next st, rib 2(5:2:5). 66(72:78:84) sts. Change to 5½mm needles.

Continue in pattern **1st row** (RS) P6(3:6:3), [K6, P6] to last 12(9:12:9) sts, K6, P6(3:6:3). **2nd and every alt row** K6(3:6:3), [P6, K6] to last 12(9:12:9) sts, P6, K6(3:6:3). **3rd row** As 1st row. **5th row** P6(3:6:3), [C6F, P6] to last 12(9:12:9) sts, C6F, P6(3:6:3). **7th row** As 1st row. **8th row** As 2nd row. These 8 rows form patt. Cont in patt until back measures 55(61:67:73)cm from beg, ending with a WS row.

Shape shoulders Cast off 9(10:11:12) sts at beg of next 4 rows. Leave rem 30(32:34:36) sts on a spare needle.

FRONT

Work as back until front measures 12(12: 14:14) rows less than back to shoulders, ending with a WS row.

Shape neck **Next row** Patt 25(28:31:34) sts, turn. Cont on these sts only for 1st side and leave rem sts on a spare needle.

Dec one st at neck edge on every row until 18(20:22:24) sts rem. Patt 4(3:4:3) rows, thus ending at side edge.

Shape shoulder Cast off 9(10:11:12) sts at beg of next row. Patt 1 row. Cast off rem 9(10:11:12) sts. With RS facing, sl centre 16 sts on to a st holder, rejoin yarn to inner end of rem sts and patt to end. Complete to match 1st side, working 1 extra row before shaping shoulder.

SLEEVES

Using 5mm needles and 1 strand of A and 1 strand of B tog, cast on 31(31:35:35) sts. Rib 11 rows as back. **Inc row** Rib 3(3:2:2), [inc in next st, rib 1, inc in next st, rib 2] 5(5:6:6) times, inc in next st, rib 2. 42(42: 48:48) sts. Change to 5½mm needles. Cont in patt as for 1st(1st:2nd:4th) size of back, inc one st at each end of 5th row and every foll 4th row, taking inc sts into patt, until there are 60(64:68:72) sts. Patt straight until work measures 29(32:35: 38)cm from beg, ending with a WS row. Cast off loosely.

COLLAR

Join right shoulder seam. With RS facing, using 5mm needles and 1 strand of A and 1 strand of B tog, K up 12(12:13:14) sts down left front neck, across sts at centre front work K5(1:1:5), [K2 tog] 3(2:2:3) times, K5(6:6:5), [K2 tog] 0(2:2:0) times, K0(1:1:0), K up 12(12:13:14) sts up right

front neck then K across sts of back neck working [K2tog] 3 times across each cable. 58(62:66:68) sts. Work 19cm in K1, P1 rib. Cast off loosely in rib.

TO MAKE UP

Join left shoulder and collar seam, reversing seam for last 12cm of collar for turn-over section. Place markers 16(17: 18:19)cm down from shoulders on back and front. Sew in sleeves between markers. Join side and sleeve seams.

LEG WARMERS

Using 5mm needles and 1 strand of A and 1 strand of B tog, cast on 29(33:37:41) sts. Rib 6cm as back, ending with a 1st rib row. **Inc row** Rib 14(5:4:2), [inc in next st, rib 14(10:6:5)] 1(2:4:6) times, inc in next 0(1:1:1)st, rib 0(5:4:2). 30(36:42:48) sts. Change to 5½mm needles. Cont in patt as back until work measures 20(23:27: 31)cm from beg, ending with a RS row. **Next row** Patt 2, [inc in next st, patt 3(4:5:6)] 6 times, inc in next st, patt 3. 37(43:49:55) sts. Rib 7cm as at beg. Cast off in rib. Join centre back seam.

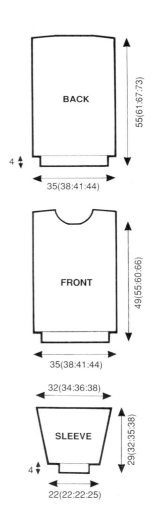

Aran Sweater

A chunky Aran sweater knitted in panels of cable and moss stitch. The big collar is knitted in rib and sewn on afterwards.

Skill Rating Medium
Sizes To fit age 6(8:10) years
To fit chest 26(28:30)in/66(71:76)cm
Actual size 72(76:82)cm
Length to shoulder 42(46:50)cm *Sleeve seam* 30(34:38)cm
Materials 12(14:16) x 50g balls of 100%
wool Aran in cream
Pair each 3¾mm and 5mm knitting needles
Cable needle
Tension 16 sts and 28 rows to 10cm over m st on 5mm needles
Special Abbreviations
C4F = sl next 2 sts on to cable needle and leave at front, K2,
then K2 from cable needle
C4B = sl next 2 sts on to cable needle and leave at back, K2
then K2 from cable needle

BACK

Using 3¾mm needles cast on 57(63:69) sts. **1st rib row** K1, [P1, K1] to end. **2nd rib row** P1, [K1, P1] to end. Rep these 2 rows until work measures 6cm from beg, ending with a 1st rib row. **Next row** Rib 10(14:16), [inc in next st] 37(35:37) times, rib as set to end. 94(98:106) sts. Change to 5mm needles.
Commence pattern **1st row** [K1, P1] 4(5:5) times, K1, P3, K8, P3, K1, P3, K40(40:48), P3, K1, P3, K8, P3, [K1, P1] 4(5:5) times, K1. **2nd and every foll alt row** [K1, P1] 4(5:5) times, P1, K3, P8, K3, P1, K3, P40(40:48), K3, P1, K3, P8, K3, P1, [P1, K1] 4(5:5) times. **3rd row** [K1, P1] 4(5:5) times, K1, P3, C4F, C4B, P3, K1, P3, [C4B, C4F] 5(5:6) times, P3, K1, P3, C4F, C4B, P3, [K1, P1] 4(5:5) times, K1. **5th row** As 1st row. **7th row** [K1, P1] 4(5:5) times, K1, P3, C4B, C4F, P3, K1, P3, [C4F, C4B] 5(5:6) times, P3, K1, P3, C4B, C4F, P3, [K1, P1] 4(5:5) times, K1. **9th row** As 1st row. **11th row** [K1, P1] 4(5:5) times, K1, P3, C4B, C4F, P3, K1, P3, [C4B, C4F] 5(5:6) times, P3, K1, P3, C4B, C4F, P3, [K1, P1] 4(5:5) times, K1. **13th row** As 1st row. **15th row** [K1, P1] 4(5:5) times, K1, P3, C4F, C4B, P3, K1, P3, [C4F, C4B] 5(5:6) times, P3, K1, P3, C4F, C4B, P3, [K1,P1] 4(5:5) times, K1. **16th row** As 2nd row. These 16 rows form patt. Cont in patt until work measures 42(46:50)cm from beg, ending with a WS row. Cast off, working K2 tog over cable panels.

FRONT

Work as given for back until front measures 26(30:34)cm from beg, ending with a WS row.
Divide for neck **Next row** Patt 25(27:27), turn. Cont on these sts only for 1st side and leave rem sts on a spare needle. Cont straight until front matches back to shoulder. Cast off, working K2 tog over cable panel. With RS facing rejoin yarn and cast off centre 44(44:52) sts working K2 tog over cable panel, patt to end. Keeping patt correct cont straight until front matches back to shoulder. Cast off, working K2 tog over cable panel.

SLEEVES

Using 3¾mm needles cast on 37(39:41) sts. **1st rib row** (RS) K1, [P1, K1] to end. **2nd rib row** P1, [K1, P1] to end. Rep these 2 rows until work measures 6cm from beg, ending with a 1st rib row. **Next row** Rib 11(7:5), * inc in next st, rib 12(7:5), rep from * to end. 39(43:47) sts. Change to 5mm needles.
Commence pattern **1st row** K1, [P1, K1] to end. **2nd row** K1, [P1, K1] to end. These 2 rows form m st patt. Cont in patt, inc one st at each end of next and every foll 5th(6th:6th) row, working inc sts into patt until there are 61(67:73) sts. Cont without shaping until sleeve measures 30(34:38)cm from beg, ending with a WS row. Cast off loosely.

COLLAR

Using 5mm needles cast on 103(103:111) sts and work 15(15:17)cm in rib as given for back. Cast off very loosely in rib.

TO MAKE UP

Press according to directions on ball band taking care not to flatten cables. Join shoulder seams. Place markers 19(21:23)cm down from shoulders on back and front. Sew in sleeves between markers. Join side and sleeve seams. Sew cast on edge of collar to neck edge. Crossing over at front, sew row ends to cast off sts at centre front.

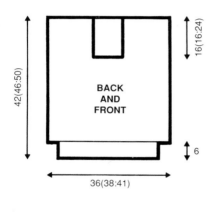

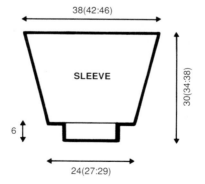

School Button-Neck Pullover

This cotton cable sweater with ribbed collar can be knitted for a boy or girl.

Skill Rating Medium
Sizes To fit age 4-6(8-10) years
To fit chest 24-26(28-30)in/61-66(71-76)cm
Actual size 73(84)cm
Length to shoulder 42(47)cm *Sleeve seam* 30(38)cm
Materials 9(10) x 50g balls of 100% cotton DK in navy or red
We used Hayfield Raw Cotton DK
Pair each of 3mm and 4mm knitting needles • Cable needle • 2 buttons
Tension 2 patt reps (16 sts) to 5·5cm measured over slightly stretched patt on
4mm needles, 28 rows to 10cm over patt on 4mm needles
Special Abbreviations
C4B = slip next 2 sts on to cable needle and hold at back,
K2 then K2 from cable needle
C4F = slip next 2 sts on to cable needle and hold at front,
K2 then K2 from cable needle

BACK

Using 3mm needles cast on 106(122) sts.
1st rib row (RS) P2, [K2, P2] to end. **2nd rib row** K2, [P2, K2] to end. Rep these 2 rows for 6(7)cm, ending with a 2nd rib row. Change to 4mm needles. **Next row** P2, [K6, P2] to end. **Next row** K2, [P6, K2] to end. Rep last 2 rows once.
Continue in pattern **1st row** (RS) P2, [C4F, K2, P2] to end. **2nd row** K2, [P6, K2] to end. **3rd row** P2, [K2, C4B, P2] to end. **4th row** K2, [P6, K2] to end. **5th to 8th rows** As 1st to 4th rows. **9th row** P2, [K6, P2] to end. **10th row** K2, [P6, K2] to end. **11th to 14th rows** Rep 9th and 10th rows twice. These 14 rows form patt. Patt straight until work measures 42(47)cm from beg, ending with a WS row.
Shape shoulders Cast off in patt 12(14) sts at beg of next 4 rows and 12(15) sts on foll 2 rows. Cast off rem 34(36) sts.

FRONT

Work as back until front measures 29 (34)cm from beg, ending with a WS row.
Divide for opening **Next row** Patt 50(58) sts, turn. Cont on these sts only for first side and leave rem sts on a spare needle. Patt straight until work measures 37(42)cm from beg, ending at inner edge.
Shape neck Cast off 6 sts at beg of next row. Dec one st at neck edge on every row until 36(43) sts rem. Patt straight until

front matches back to shoulder, ending at side edge.
Shape shoulder Cast off 12(14) sts at beg of next row and foll alt row. Patt 1 row. Cast off rem 12(15) sts. With RS of work facing rejoin yarn to inner end of sts on spare needle, cast off 6 sts, patt to end. Complete to match first side.

SLEEVES

Using 3mm needles cast on 50 sts. Rib 4(5)cm as given for back, ending with a 2nd rib row. Change to 4mm needles.
Next row (RS) P2, [K6, P2] to end. **Next row** K2, [P6, K2] to end. **Next row** Inc in first st, P1, [K6, P2] to last 8 sts, K6, P1, inc in last st. 52 sts. **Next row** P1, [K2, P6] to last 3 sts, K2, P1. These 4 rows set position of patt. Cont in patt to match back working first cables in next row and inc one st at each end of every RS row, taking inc sts into patt, until there are 98(104) sts, then at each end of every foll 2nd(3rd) row until there are 110(122) sts. Patt straight until work measures 30(38)cm from beg, ending with a WS row. Cast off loosely in patt.

BUTTON BAND

With RS of work facing and 3mm needles, K up 22 sts up right front opening edge for a boy or left front opening edge for a girl.
1st rib row (WS) P2, [K2, P2] to end. **2nd rib row** K2, [P2, K2] to end. Rep last 2

rows 3 times, then work 1st rib row again. Cast off in rib.

BUTTONHOLE BAND

Knitting sts up along other front opening edge, work as given for button band until 3 rows of rib have been worked.
1st buttonhole row (RS) Rib 4, cast off next 2 sts, rib 9 including st rem on needle after casting off, cast off next 2 sts, rib to end. **2nd buttonhole row** Rib to end casting on 2 sts over those cast off on previous row. Rib 4 rows. Cast off in rib.

COLLAR

Join shoulder seams. With RS of work facing and 3mm needles, beg at centre of front band and K up 27(28) sts up right front neck, 34(36) sts across back neck and 27(28) sts down left front neck to centre of front band. 88(92) sts. **1st rib row** (RS of collar) K3, [P2, K2] to last st, K1. **2nd rib row** K1, [P2, K2] to last 3 sts, P2, K1. Rep last 2 rows for 6cm. Cast off loosely in rib.

TO MAKE UP

Press lightly according to directions on ball band. Place markers 19(21)cm down from shoulders on back and front. Sew in sleeves between markers. Join side and sleeve seams. Overlap front bands and join ends to cast-off sts at centre front. Sew on buttons to correspond to buttonholes.

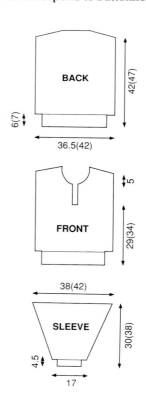

Spanish Bolero

This stylish bolero top has shaped fronts and is knitted in simple all over moss-stitch pattern.

Skill Rating Easy
Sizes To fit age 6(8:10:12) years
To fit chest 26(28:30:32)in/66(71:76:81)cm
Actual size 74(80:85:90)cm
Length to shoulder 32(35:40:45)cm *Sleeve seam* 23(25:26:28)cm
Materials 5(6:6:7) x 50g balls of
80% wool/20% Bri-Nylon DK in red
We used Wendy Ascot DK
Pair of 4mm knitting needles • 2½mm crochet hook
Tension 23 sts and 39 rows to 10cm over
moss-stitch on 4mm needles

BACK

Using 4mm needles cast on 86(92: 98:104) sts. **1st row** [K1, P1] to end. **2nd row** [P1, K1] to end. These 2 rows form m-st patt. Cont in patt until work measures 14(16:20:24)cm.

Shape armholes Cast off 6(6:8:8) sts at beg of next 2 rows. 74(80:82:88) sts. Cont straight in patt until work measures 32(35:40:45)cm from beg.

Shape shoulders Cast off 10(11:11:12) sts at beg of next 4 rows. Cast off rem 34(36:38:40) sts.

LEFT FRONT

Using 4mm needles cast on 15(18:21:24) sts. Work 1 row m st.

Shape front edge Cast on 5 sts at beg of next row, 3 sts at beg of foll alt row and 2 sts at beg of foll 3 alt rows. 29(32:35:38) sts. Inc one st at shaped front edge on every foll alt row until there are 41(44:47: 50) sts, then inc on next 2(2:3:2) foll 4th rows. 43(46:50:52) sts. Cont straight in patt until front measures same as back to armholes, ending at side edge.

Shape armhole Cast off 6(6:8:8) sts at beg of next row. 37(40:42:44) sts. Cont straight in patt until front measures 19 (22:25:28)cm from beg, ending at front edge.

Shape neck Dec one st at neck edge on next and every foll 3rd row until 30(32:32:34) sts rem. Dec one st at neck edge on every alt row until 20(22:22:24) sts rem. Cont in patt without shaping until front matches back to shoulder, ending at armhole edge.

Shape shoulder Cast off 10(11:11:12) sts at beg of next row. Work 1 row. Cast off rem 10(11:11:12) sts.

RIGHT FRONT

Using 4mm needles cast on 15(18:21:24) sts. Work 2 rows m st.

Shape front edge Cast on 5 sts at beg of next row, 3 sts at beg of foll alt row and 2 sts at beg of foll 3 alt rows. 29(32:35:38) sts. Inc one st at shaped front edge on every foll alt row until there are 41(44:47: 50) sts, then inc on next 2(2:3:2) foll 4th rows. 43(46:50:52) sts. Cont straight in patt until front measures same as back to armholes, ending at side edge.

Shape armhole Cast off 6(6:8:8) sts at beg of next row. 37(40:42:44) sts. Cont straight in patt until front measures 19 (22:25:28)cm from beg, ending at front edge.

Shape neck Dec one st at neck edge on next and every foll 3rd row until 30(32:32:34) sts rem. Dec one st at neck edge on every alt row until 20(22:22:24) sts rem. Cont in patt without shaping until front matches back to shoulder, ending at armhole edge.

Shape shoulder Cast off 10(11:11:12) sts at beg of next row. Work 1 row. Cast off rem 10(11:11:12) sts.

SLEEVES

Using 4mm needles cast on 52(56:60:64) sts. Work in m-st, inc one st at each end of every 4th(5th:5th:6th) row until there

are 84(90:94:98) sts. Cont without shaping until sleeve measures 25(27:29:31)cm. Cast off loosely.

TO MAKE UP

Press according to directions on the ball band. Join shoulder seams. Sew in sleeves to armhole, setting them in squarely and sewing last 2(2:3:3)cm of side edges of sleeves to cast off sts at armholes. Join side and sleeve seams.

Edging Beginning and ending at left side seam, using 2½mm crochet hook and with RS facing, work 1 round DC all around front edges, then work 1 more round DC but working clockwise so that the round is worked backwards and a twisted border is formed. (This stitch is sometimes called crab stitch). Work edgings around each cuff.

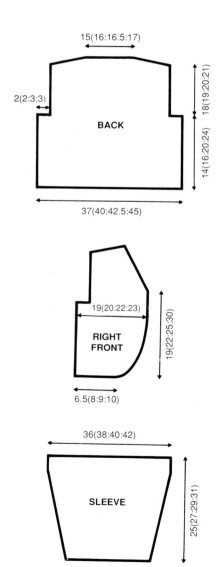

Striped V-Neck Sweater

An easy striped sweater knitted in stocking stitch. The wrap-over collar is knitted in rib.

Skill Rating Easy
Sizes To fit age 2(4:6:8:10) years
To fit chest 22(24:26:28:30)in/56(61:66:71:76)cm
Actual size 62(67:72:77:82)cm
Length to shoulder 39(43:49:51:54)cm *Sleeve seam* 24(31:37:41:42)cm
Materials 3(3:4:4:5) x 50g balls of 100% wool DK in navy (colour A)
and 2(2:3:4:4) balls same in green (B)
We used Sunbeam Pure New Wool DK
Pair each of 3¼mm and 4mm knitting needles
3¼mm circular knitting needle
Tension 24 sts and 30 rows to 10cm over st st on 4mm needles

BACK

Using 3¼mm needles and A, cast on 75(81:87:93:99) sts. **1st rib row** (RS) K1, * P1, K1, rep from * to end. **2nd rib row** P1, * K1, P1, rep from * to end. Rep these 2 rows for 5cm ending with a 2nd rib row, inc one st at end of last row. 76(82:88:94:100) sts. Change to 4mm needles. Beg with a K row cont in st st in stripe patt as folls, carrying yarn not in use loosely up side of work: Using B work 10 rows, using A work 10 rows. These 20 rows form patt **. Cont in patt until work measures 34(38:44:46:49)cm from beg, ending with a P row.

Shape neck **Next row** K26(27:28: 30:32), turn and leave rem sts on a spare needle. Cast off 2 sts at beg of next and foll 1(1:2:2:2) alt rows. Dec one st at same edge on every alt row until 19(20: 20:22:24) sts rem. Cont without shaping until work measures 39(43:49:51:54)cm, ending at side edge.

Shape shoulder Cast off 10(10:10:11: 12) sts at beg of next row. Work 1 row. Cast off rem 9(10:10:11:12) sts. With RS of work facing, return to sts on spare needle. Sl first 24(28:32:34:36) sts onto a holder. Join yarn to rem sts and K to end. Complete to match first side of neck.

FRONT

Work as given for back to **. Cont in patt until work measures 23(26:31:32:34)cm from beg, ending with a P row.

Shape neck **Next row** K34(37:39:42: 45), turn and leave rem sts on a spare needle. Dec one st at neck edge on every foll alt row until 26(29:31:34:37) sts rem. Dec one st at neck edge on every foll 3rd row until 19(20:20:22:24) sts rem. Cont without shaping until front matches back to shoulder, ending at side edge.

Shape shoulder Cast off 10(10:10: 11:12) sts at beg of next row. Work 1 row. Cast off rem 9(10:10:11:12) sts. With RS of work facing, join yarn to rem sts, cast off first 8(8:10:10:10) sts, K to end. Complete to match first side of neck.

SLEEVES

Using 3¼mm needles and A, cast on 37(39:41:43:45) sts and work 5cm in rib as for back, ending with a 1st row. **Inc row** Rib 4(5:6:7:8), * M1, rib 10, rep from * to last 3(4:5:6:7) sts, M1, rib to end. 41(43: 45:47:49) sts. Change to 4mm needles. Cont in patt as for back, inc one st at each end of 1st (13th:1st: 1st:1st) and every foll 4th(4th:6th: 6th:6th) row until there are 67(71:75: 81:85) sts. Cont without shaping until work measures 24(31:37:41:42)cm, ending with a P row. Cast off 10 sts at beg of next 4 rows. Cast off.

COLLAR

Join shoulder seams. With RS of work facing, using 3¼mm circular needle and A, K up 54(60:64:68:70) sts up right front neck, 18 sts down right back neck, K across sts of back neck dec one st at centre, K up 18 sts up left back neck then 54(60:64:68:70) sts down left front neck.

167(183:195:205:211) sts. Working backwards and forwards in rows, work 3.5(3.5:4.5:4.5:4.5)cm in K1, P1 rib as given for back. Cast off in rib.

TO MAKE UP

Fold left side of collar over right, and sew row ends to cast off sts at centre front. Place markers 14(14.5:15.5:17:17.5)cm down from shoulders on back and front. Sew in sleeves between markers. Join side and sleeve seams.

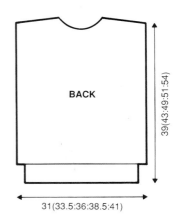

BACK

39(43:49:51:54)

31(33.5:36:38.5:41)

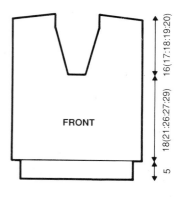

FRONT

16(17:18:19:20)

18(21:26:27:29)

5

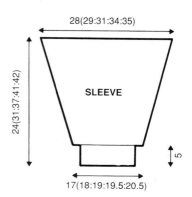

28(29:31:34:35)

SLEEVE

24(31:37:41:42)

5

17(18:19:19.5:20.5)

Boys' Slipover

Kit him out in our super slipover.

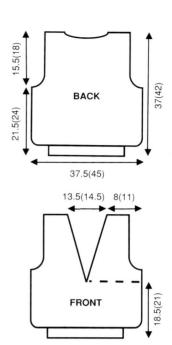

Skill Rating Medium
Sizes To fit age 3-5(6-8) years
Actual size 75(90)cm
Length to shoulder 37(42)cm
Materials 3(4) x 50g balls of 55% wool/25% acrylic/20% nylon
DK in natural (colour A), and 1 ball each of same in navy, jade,
scarlet, royal and yellow
We used Patons Diploma Gold DK
Pair each of 3¼mm and 4mm knitting needles
Tension 24 sts and 24 rows to 10cm over st st on 4mm needles

BACK

Using 3¼mm needles and A, cast on
73(83) sts. **1st rib row** (RS) K1, [P1, K1]
to end. **2nd rib row** P1, [K1, P1] to end.
Rep these 2 rows for 4cm, ending with a
1st rib row. **Next row** Rib 3(4), [M1, rib
4(3)] 17(25) times, M1, rib 2(4). 91(109)
sts. Change to 4mm needles. Cont in st st
from chart, reading odd-numbered rows
from right to left and even-numbered
rows from left to right. Work 42(48) rows
ending with a WS row.
    Shape armholes Keeping patt correct,
cast off 3 sts at beg of next 2 rows and 2
sts on foll 2 rows. Dec one st at each end of
next 4(6) RS rows. 73(87) sts. Cont straight
until a total of 74(86) patt rows have been
completed, ending with a WS row.
    Shape neck **Next row** Patt 25(31), cast
off next 23(25) sts, patt to end. Cont on
last set of sts only. Patt 1 row. Cast off 5
sts at beg of next row. Patt 1 row. Cast off
rem 20(26) sts. With WS facing, rejoin
yarn to inner end of rem sts and
complete to match.

FRONT

Work as given for back until 35(41) rows
of patt have been completed, ending with
a RS row.
    Divide for neck **Next row** (WS) Patt
45(54) sts, turn. Cont on these sts only
leaving rem 46(55) sts on a spare needle.
Dec one st at neck edge of every RS row
until front matches back to armhole,
ending at side edge.
    Shape armhole Still dec at neck
edge, cast off 3 sts at beg of next row and
2 sts on the foll alt row, then dec one st
at armhole edge on next 4(6) RS rows.
Cont to dec at neck edge only until

20(26) sts rem. Patt straight until front
matches back to shoulder. Cast off. With
WS facing, return to sts on spare needle,
cast off centre st, patt to end. Complete
to match 1st side.

NECKBAND

Join right shoulder seam. Using 3¼mm
needles and A and with RS facing, K up
42(48) sts down left front neck, one st
from centre, 42(48) sts up right front
neck and 32(34) sts around back neck.
117(131) sts. **1st row** P1, [K1, P1] to
end. **2nd row** [K1, P1] 20(23) times,
K2 tog tbl, K1, K2 tog, [P1, K1] to end.
3rd row P1, [K1, P1] 35(39) times, P2
tog, P1, P2 tog tbl, P1, [K1, P1] to end.
Cont in this way, dec one st at either
side of centre st, for a further 3 rows.
Cast off in rib, dec as before.

ARMBANDS

Join left shoulder and neckband seam.
With RS facing, 3¼mm needles and A, K
up 73(83) sts evenly around armhole. Rib
6 rows as at beg of back. Cast off in rib.

TO MAKE UP

Join side seams and ends of armbands.

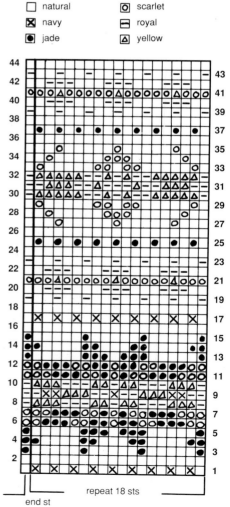

☐	natural	◧	scarlet
☒	navy	⊟	royal
◉	jade	△	yellow

repeat 18 sts

end st

Rope Cable Cardigan

A generously sized cable cardigan knitted in pure cotton. The bands are worked all in one with the fronts.

Skill Rating Medium
Sizes To fit age 1-2(4-6:8-10) years
To fit chest 20-22(24-26:28-30)in/51-56(61-66:71-76)cm
Actual size 63(76:90)cm
Length to shoulder 37(44:51)cm *Sleeve seam* 23(29:35)cm
Materials 6(7:9) x 50g balls of 100% cotton DK in blue
We used Hayfield Raw Cotton DK
A pair each of 3¼mm and 4mm knitting needles • Cable needle • 5 buttons
Tension 26 sts and 30 rows to 10cm over patt on 4mm needles
Special Abbreviation
C6F = slip next 3 sts onto cable needle and leave at front,
K3, then K3 from cable needle

BACK

Using 3¼mm needles cast on 73(89:105) sts. **1st rib row** K1, [P1, K1] to end. **2nd rib row** P1, [K1, P1] to end. Rep these 2 rows for 6cm, ending with a 2nd row. **Next row** Rib 5, [M1, rib 8] 8(10:12) times, M1, rib 4. 82(100:118) sts. Change to 4mm needles. **Foundation row** K2, [P6, K3] 8(10:12) times, P6, K2.

Commence pattern **1st row** (RS) K2, [C6F, K3] 8(10:12) times, C6F, K2. **2nd and every foll alt row** K2, [P6, K3] 8(10:12) times, P6, K2. **3rd, 5th and 7th rows** K. **8th row** As 2nd row. These 8 rows form patt. Cont in patt until back measures 37(44:51)cm from beg, ending with a 6th patt row. Cast off.

RIGHT FRONT

Note that the front bands are knitted in with patt. Using 3¼mm needles cast on 39(47:55) sts. **1st row** K9, [K1, P1] to end. **2nd row** [K1, P1] to last 9 sts, K9. Rep these 2 rows for 6cm, ending with a 2nd row. **Next row** K9, rib 1(4:2), [M1, rib 7(6:7) sts] 4(5:6) times, M1, rib to end. 44(53:62) sts. Change to 4mm needles but cont working g-st band on 3¼mm needles. **Foundation row** K2, [P6, K3] 3(4:5) times, P6, K9.

Commence pattern **1st row** (RS) K9, [C6F, K3] 3(4:5) times, C6F, K2. **2nd and every foll alt row** K2, [P6, K3] 3(4:5) times, P6, K9. **3rd, 5th and 7th rows** K. **8th row** As 2nd row. These 8 rows form patt. Cont in patt until front measures 31(38:45)cm, ending WS row. (For left front, ending RS row).

Shape neck **Next row** K9, sl these sts onto a holder, cast off 2(4:6) sts, patt to end. Keeping patt correct, dec one st at neck edge on every row until 20(27:36) sts rem. Cont without shaping until front matches back. Cast off. Mark 4 button positions on the band, the first 4 rows up from cast on edge, the last 7(9:11)cm below front neck, the rest spaced evenly between.

LEFT FRONT

Using 3¼mm needles cast on 39(47:55) sts. **1st row** [K1, P1] to last 9 sts, K9. **2nd row** K9, rib to end. Rep these 2 rows once more. **Buttonhole row** (RS) Rib to last 9 sts, K2, sl 1, K1, psso, cast on 2 sts, K2 tog, K3. Rep 2nd and 1st rows until work measures 6cm from beg, ending with a 2nd row. **Next row** Rib 1(4:2), [M1, rib 7(6:7) sts] 4(5:6) times, M1, rib 1(4:2), K9. 44(53:62) sts. Change to 4mm needles but cont working g-st band on 3¼mm needles. **Foundation row** K9, [P6, K3] 3(4:5) times, P6, K2.

Commence pattern **1st row** (RS) K2, [C6F, K3] 3(4:5) times, C6F, K9. **2nd and every foll alt row** K9, [P6, K3] 3(4:5) times, P6, K2. **3rd, 5th and 7th rows** K. **8th row** As 2nd row. Complete to match right front, making buttonholes as before to match markers on band.

SLEEVES

Using 3¼mm needles cast on 33(41:49) sts and work 3cm rib as given for back, ending with a 2nd row. **Next row** Rib 5(1:4), [M1, rib 2(3:3) sts] 12(13:14) times, M1, rib to end. 46(55:64) sts. Change to 4mm needles. **Foundation row** K2, [P6, K3] 4(5:6) times, P6, K2. Work in patt as given for back but rep instructions in square brackets 4(5:6) times. Inc and work into patt one st at each end of 3rd and every foll 2nd(3rd:4th) row until there are 62(91:104) sts, then every foll 3rd(4th: 6th) row until there are 88(101:108) sts. Cont without shaping until sleeve measures 23(29:35)cm from beg, ending with a WS row. Cast off.

NECKBAND

Join shoulder seams. Using 3¼mm needles and with RS facing, K9 sts from right front band, K up 20(22:24) sts up right front neck, 37(41:41) sts across back neck, 20(22:24) sts down left front neck, K9 sts from left front band. 95(103:107) sts. K3 rows. **Next row** K to last 7 sts, sl1, K1, psso, cast on 2 sts, K2 tog, K3. K4 rows. Cast off.

TO MAKE UP

Press according to directions on ball band. Place markers 17(19.5:21)cm down from shoulders on back and fronts for arm-holes. Sew in sleeves between markers. Join side and sleeve seams. Sew on buttons to match buttonholes.

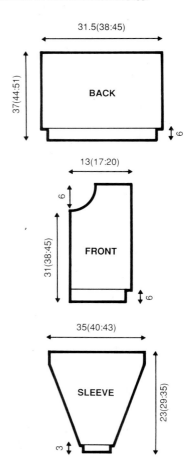

Kids' Jacket and Beret

Skill Rating Medium
Sizes To fit age 2(4:6:8) years
Jacket: To fit chest 22(24:26:28)in/56(61:66:71)cm
Actual size 80(85:90:97)cm
Length to shoulder 40(45:49:54)cm *Sleeve seam* 24(28:32:36)cm
Beret: To fit age 2-4(6-8) years
Materials *Jacket* 10(11:12:13) x 50g balls
of 100% wool Chunky in gold or plum
Beret 2 balls same
We used Jaeger Matchmaker Sport
Pair each of 4mm and 4¹/₂mm knitting needles
Set of four double-pointed 4¹/₂mm knitting needles for beret
4(5:5:5) buttons
Tension 17 sts and 32 rows to 10cm over m st on 4¹/₂mm needles

JACKET

BACK

Using 4mm needles, cast on 64(68:72:76) sts.
Work in m st **1st row** (RS) [K1, P1] to end. **2nd row** [P1, K1] to end. These 2 rows form m st. Change to 4¹/₂mm needles and cont in m st until back measures 39(44:48:53)cm from beg, ending with a WS row.
Neck and shoulder shaping **Next row** M st 25(26:27:28), turn. Cont on these sts only for 1st side and leave rem sts on a spare needle. Dec one st at neck edge on next 2 rows. Work 1 row. Cast off rem 23(24:25:26) sts. With RS facing, rejoin yarn to inner end of rem sts, cast off 14(16:18:20) sts, m st to end. Complete to match 1st side.

POCKET LININGS

Make 2 Using 4¹/₂mm needles, cast on 16 sts. Beg with a K row, work 10cm in st st, ending with a P row. Leave sts on a spare needle.

LEFT FRONT

Using 4mm needles, cast on 34(36:38:42) sts. M st 2 rows. Change to 4¹/₂mm needles and cont in m st until work measures 14(16:18:20)cm from beg, ending with a WS row.
Pocket opening row M st 7(7:7:9), sl next 16 sts on to a holder, m st across sts of one pocket lining, m st 11(13:15:17). Cont in m st until work measures 35(40:44:49)cm from beg, ending with a RS row.
Shape neck Cast off 6 sts at beg of next

row and 2 sts on foll alt row. Dec one st at neck edge on every row until 23(24:25:26) sts rem. Cont straight until front measures same as back to shoulder, ending with a WS row. Cast off.

RIGHT FRONT

Work to match left front, reversing pocket opening row and ending with a WS row before shaping neck.

SLEEVES

Using 4mm needles, cast on 32(36:36:40) sts. M st 2 rows. Change to 4¹/₂mm needles and cont in m st until work measures 5cm, ending with a RS row.
Next row (WS) P to mark fold line. Cont in m st, inc one st at each end of 5th and every foll 5th(6th:7th:7th) row until there are 58(62:64:68) sts. Cont straight until sleeve measures 24(28:32:36)cm from fold line. Cast off loosely in m st.

COLLAR

Using 4mm needles, cast on 61(65:69:73) sts. **1st rib row** (RS) K1, [P1, K1] to end. **2nd rib row** P1, [K1, P1] to end. Change to 4¹/₂mm needles. Rep 2nd rib row only, to form m st, and cont until collar measures 6(6:7:8)cm from beg. Cast off in m st.

POCKET FLAPS

With RS facing and 4mm needles, work 6 rows in m st across sts of pocket. K 1 row to mark fold line. M st 6 rows. Cast off in m st.

BUTTONHOLE BAND

With RS facing and 4mm needles, K up 64(70:76:82) sts evenly up straight edge of right front. Work 2 rows in K1, P1 rib.
1st buttonhole row (WS) Rib 5, [cast off next 2 sts, rib next 14(11:12:14) sts] 3(4:4:4) times, cast off next 2 sts, rib to end. **2nd buttonhole row** Rib to end, casting on 2 sts over each cast-off group. Rib 2 rows. Cast off in rib.

BUTTON BAND

With RS facing and 4mm needles, K up 64(70:76:82) sts evenly down straight edge of left front. Work 6 rows in P1, K1 rib. Cast off in rib.

TO MAKE UP

Join shoulder seams. Leaving front bands free, sew cast-on edge of collar to neck edge. Mark position of underarms 17(18:19:20)cm down from shoulders on back and fronts. Sew on sleeves between markers. Join side seams. Join sleeve seams, reversing first 6cm for turn-back cuffs. Fold pocket flaps on to RS along fold line and sew ends in place. Sew down pocket linings neatly on WS. Sew on buttons.

BERET

Using 4mm needles, cast on 70(88) sts. Work 3cm in K1, P1 rib. **Inc row** Rib 3(6), [inc in next st, rib 1(2)] to last 5(7) sts, inc in next st, rib 4(6). 102(114) sts. Sl 34(38) sts on to each of 3 double-pointed 4¹/₂mm needles. *Cont in rounds of m st* **1st m st round** [K1, P1] to end. **2nd m st round** [P1, K1] to end. Rep these 2 rounds 6 times more. *Cont in st st* **Inc round** [K9(18), inc in next st] to last 2(0) sts, K2(0). 112(120) sts. K 4 rounds.
Shape crown **1st round** [K12(13), K 2 tog] 8 times. **2nd round** K. **3rd round** [K11(12), K 2 tog] 8 times. **4th round** K. **5th round** [K10(11), K 2 tog] 8 times. **6th round** K. Cont in this way, working one st less before each dec on every alt round until 16 sts rem. **Next round** [K2 tog] to end. Cut yarn leaving a 50cm end, thread end through rem 8 sts, draw up and secure. Do not fasten off.
To make stalk Wrap yarn 3 times around 2 fingers at beret end of yarn, sew ends of loops to centre of beret then wind yarn tightly around entire length of doubled loops. Fasten off securely. Join ends of rib.

Fair Isle Sweater

This round neck sweater has a pretty collar finished with a picot edge.

Skill Rating Experienced
Sizes To fit age 2(4:6:8:10) years
To fit chest 22(24:26:28:30)in/56(61:66:71:76)cm
Actual size 63(70:77:81:88)cm
Length to shoulder 35(38:41:45:49)cm *Sleeve seam* 26(30:33:37:40)cm
Materials 4(4:4:5:5) x 50g balls of 100% cotton DK in natural or navy (colour A) and 1(1:1:2:2) balls same in mauve (B), pink (C), kingfisher (D) and sand (E)
We used Hayfield Raw Cotton DK
Pair each 3¼mm and 4½mm knitting needles
Tension 22 sts and 23 rows to 10cm over patt on 4½mm needles.
Note: When working Fair Isle pattern it is essential to maintain an even tension. Spread stitches on right hand needle before changing colours, then strand the second colour loosely across the back of the work before knitting with it. Do not pull tightly or the work will pucker and the tension will distort. Do not weave in yarns or the fabric will thicken and the tension will change.

14(16:17:19:20)cm down from shoulders on back and front. Sew in sleeves between markers. Join side and sleeve seams. Sew cast-on edge of collar to neck edge, join first 4 rows at centre front neck.

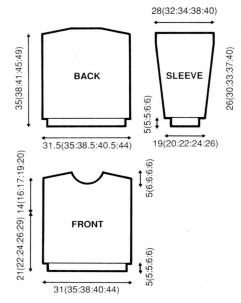

BACK

Using 3¼mm needles and A, cast on 66 (72:78:84:90) sts. **1st and every rib row** [K1, P1] to end. Rep this row for 5(5: 5:6:6)cm, ending with a RS row. **Next row** Rib 16(12:9:14:12), * M1, rib 17(12:10: 14:11), rep from * to last 16(12:9:14:12) sts, M1, rib to end. 69(77:85:89:97) sts. Change to 4½mm needles. Cont in patt from chart reading odd-numbered (K) rows from right to left and even-numbered (P) rows from left to right. **1st row** K first 4 sts of chart, rep centre 4 sts 15(17:19:20: 22) times, patt last 5 sts. **2nd row** P first 5 sts, rep centre 4 sts 15(17:19:20:22) times, patt last 4 sts. Cont in this way rep 32 chart rows until back measures 35(38:41:45: 49)cm from beg, ending with a WS row.
Shape shoulders Cast off 10(12:13:14: 15) sts at beg of next 2 rows and 10(11:13: 13:15) sts at beg of foll 2 rows. Cast off rem 29(31:33:35:37) sts.

FRONT

Work as back until front measures 30 (32:35:39:43)cm from beg, ending with a WS row.
Shape neck **Next row** Patt 27(31: 33:35:38) sts, turn and leave rem sts on a spare needle. Dec one st at neck edge on every row until 20(23:26:27:30) sts rem. Cont without shaping until front matches back to shoulder, ending at side edge.
Shape shoulder Cast off 10(12:13:14: 15) sts at beg of next row. Work 1 row. Cast off rem 10(11:13:13:15) sts. With RS

facing, rejoin yarn, cast off centre 15(15: 19:19:21) sts, patt to end. Work to match other side of neck.

SLEEVES

Using 3¼mm needles and A, cast on 38(42:46:46:50) sts. Work 5(5:5:6:6)cm K1, P1 rib as given for back, ending with a RS row. **Next row** Rib 10(11:12:5:7), * M1, rib 9(10:11:6:6), rep from * to last 10(11:12:5:7) sts, M1, rib to end. 41(45:49:53:57) sts. Change to 4½mm needles and cont in patt as for back, inc one st at each end of 3rd and every foll 4th row working inc sts into patt, until there are 63(71:77:85:89) sts. Cont without shaping until work measures 26(30:33:37:40)cm, ending with a WS row. Cast off loosely in A.

COLLAR

Using 3¼mm needles and A, cast on 97 (97:107:107:117) sts. **1st row** K1, [P1, K1] to end. **2nd row** P1, [K1, P1] to end. Rep these 2 rows until work measures 6.5cm, ending with a 1st row. When A is natural change to C, when A is navy change to D and P1 row. **Next row** Cast off 2, * sl st on right hand needle back to left hand needle, cast on 2 sts, then cast off 5, rep from * until no more sts rem, fasten off.

TO MAKE UP

Press according to directions on ball band. Join shoulder seams. Place markers

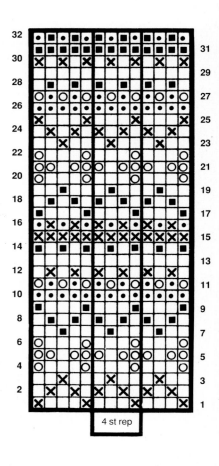

	A		C		E
	B		D		

Girls' Summer Cardigan

Skill Rating Medium
Sizes To fit age 4(6:8) years
To fit chest 24(26:28)in/61(66:71)cm
Actual size 65(77:89)cm
Length to shoulder 42(47:52)cm *Sleeve seam* 31(35:39)cm
Materials 6(7:8) x 50g balls of 100% cotton DK in white
We used Sirdar Soft Cotton DK
Pair each 3¼mm and 4mm knitting needles • 5(6:6) buttons
Tension 20 sts and 28 rows to 10cm over st st on 4mm needles

BACK

Using 3¼mm needles cast on 59(71:83) sts. **1st rib row** (RS) K1, [P1, K1] to end. **2nd rib row** P1, [K1, P1] to end. Rep these 2 rows 4(5:6) times more, then work 1st rib row again. **Inc row** Rib 4(5:6), [inc in next st, rib 9(11:13)] to last 5(6:7) sts, inc in next st, rib 4(5:6). 65(77:89) sts. Change to 4mm needles. Beg K row, st st 6 rows.
Work zigzag pattern **1st row** (RS) K2, [yo, skpo, K10] to last 3 sts, yo, skpo, K1. **2nd and every WS row** P. **3rd row** K2, [K1, yo, skpo, K7, K2 tog, yo] to last 3 sts, K3. **5th row** K2, [K2, yo, skpo, K5, K2 tog, yo, K1] to last 3 sts, K3. **7th row** K2, [K3, yo, skpo, K3, K2 tog, yo, K2] to last 3 sts, K3. **9th row** K2, [K4, yo, skpo, K1, K2 tog, yo, K3] to last 3 sts, K3. **11th row** K2, [K5, yo, sl 1, K2 tog, psso, yo, K4] to last 3 sts, K3. **13th row** K2, [K6, yo, skpo, K4] to last 3 sts, K3. **14th row** P. These 14 rows form zigzag patt. St st 12(16:20) rows. Rep 1st to 12th rows of zigzag patt.
Work faggot lace pattern **1st row** (RS) K2, [K2, yo, skpo] to last 3 sts, K3. **2nd row** K2, P1, [P2, yrn, P2 tog] to last 2 sts, K2. These 2 rows form faggot lace patt. Rep these 2 rows 7(9:11) times more. Rep 14 rows of zigzag patt. Cont in st st until back measures 42(47:52)cm from beg, ending with a P row.
Shape shoulders Cast off 20(24:28) sts at beg of next 2 rows. Leave rem 25(29:33) sts on a holder.

POCKET LININGS

Make 2 Using 4mm needles cast on 17(19:21) sts. Beg with a K row, st st 26(28:30) rows. Leave sts on a holder.

LEFT FRONT

Using 3¼mm needles cast on 27(33:39) sts. Rib 12(14:16) rows as back, inc 2 sts evenly across last row. 29(35:41) sts.

Change to 4mm needles. St st 6 rows. Work zigzag pattern *1st and 3rd sizes only* Work 14 rows as back. *2nd size only* **1st row** (RS) K2, [yo, skpo, K10] twice, yo, skpo, K7. **2nd and every WS row** P. **3rd row** K2, [K1, yo, skpo, K7, K2 tog, yo] twice, K1, yo, skpo, K6. With sts as set, patt a further 11 rows to match back.
All sizes St st 6(8:10) rows. **Pocket row** (RS) K6(8:10), sl next 17(19:21) sts on to a holder, K across 17(19:21) sts of 1st pocket lining, K6(8:10). Beg with a P row, st st 5(7:9) rows. Rep 1st to 12th rows of zigzag patt. Work 16(20:24) rows in faggot lace patt as back, but for 2nd size only, work 1 extra st in g st at each end of every row. Rep 14 rows of zigzag patt. Cont in st st until front measures 19(19: 21) rows less than back to shoulder, ending at front edge.
Shape neck Cast off 3(5:7) sts at beg of next row. Dec one st at neck edge on next 6 alt rows. 20(24:28) sts. Work 6(6:8) rows straight, ending at side edge. Cast off.

RIGHT FRONT

Work to match left front, reversing neck shaping and setting zigzag patt for 2nd size as follows **1st row** (RS) K8, [yo, skpo, K10] twice, yo, skpo, K1.

SLEEVES

Using 3¼mm needles cast on 39(43:47) sts. Rib 12(14:16) rows as back, inc 2 sts evenly across last row. 41(45:49) sts. Change to 4mm needles. K1 row. P1 row. Cont in zigzag pattern **1st row** (RS) K2 (4:6), [yo, skpo, K10] 3 times, yo, skpo, K1(3:5). With sts as set, patt 13 rows to match back, at the same time, inc and take into patt one st at each end of patt rows 5, 9 and 13. 47(51:55) sts. St st 12(16:20) rows, inc on every 4th row from previous inc. 53(59:65) sts. Cont in zigzag pattern **1st row** (RS) K8(11:2), [yo, skpo, K10] 3(3:5) times, yo, skpo, K7(10:1). With sts

as set, patt 11 rows to match back, inc on every 4th row from previous inc. 59(65:71) sts. Cont in faggot lace pattern. **1st row** (RS) K3(4:5), [K2, yo, skpo] to last 4(5:6) sts, K4(5:6). **2nd row** K3(4:5), P1, [P2, yrn, P2 tog] to last 3(4:5) sts, K3(4:5). These 2 rows form faggot lace patt. Patt a further 14(18:22) rows in faggot lace patt, inc as before and taking inc sts into patt. 67(75:83) sts. Keeping patt in alignment, work 14 rows zigzag patt. Cont in st st until sleeve measures 31(35:39)cm from beg, ending with a P row. Cast off loosely.

BUTTON BAND

Using 3¼mm needles cast on 9 sts. Work in rib as at beg of back until band, when slightly stretched, fits up left front to beg of neck shaping, ending with a WS row. Leave sts on a holder. Sew in place. Mark positions for 5(6:6) buttons on button band. The 1st 2cm from lower edge, then allowing for the last on the 3rd row of the neckband, space rem 3(4:4) evenly between.

BUTTONHOLE BAND

Work to match button band working buttonholes to correspond to markers thus: **1st buttonhole row** (RS) Rib 4, cast off 2 sts, rib to end. **2nd buttonhole row** Rib to end casting on 2 sts over those cast off on previous row. End with a RS row before leaving sts on holder.

NECKBAND

Join shoulder seams. With RS facing, sl sts of buttonhole band on to a 3¼mm needle with point to left, K up 18(20: 22) sts up right front neck, K across 25 (29:33) sts of back neck, K up 18(20:22) sts down left front neck then rib across 9 sts of button band. 79(87:95) sts. **Next row** P1, [K1, P1] to end. Work 1st and 2nd buttonhole rows. Rib 4 rows. Cast off in rib.

POCKET TOPS

With RS facing and 3¼mm needles, rib 6 rows across sts of pocket. Cast off in rib.

TO MAKE UP

Mark position of underarms 17(19:21)cm down from shoulders on back and fronts. Sew on sleeves between markers. Join side and sleeve seams. Sew down pocket linings on WS and ends of pocket tops on RS. Sew on buttons to complete.

Classic Cricket Sweater

A cabled cricket sweater with a V neck and long sleeves. The ribs are trimmed with a two colour stripe.

Skill Rating Experienced
Sizes To fit age 2(4:6:8:10) years
To fit chest 22(24:26:28:30)in/56(61:66:71:76)cm
Actual size 65(70:76:81:87)cm
Length to shoulder 36(40:44:48:52)cm *Sleeve seam* 26(29:32:35:38)cm
Materials 6(7:7:8:9) x 50g balls of 45% acrylic/40% Bri-Nylon/15% wool DK in jade or white (colour A), 1 ball same in white or jade (B) and 1 ball same in navy (C)
We used Hayfield Grampian DK
Pair each 3¼mm and 4mm knitting needles • Cable needle
Tension 29 sts and 30 rows to 10cm over patt on 4mm needles
Special Abbreviations
C6F = slip next 3 sts on to cable needle, hold at front of work, K3, then K3 sts from cable needle
C3F = slip next 2 sts on to cable needle, hold at front of work, P1, then K2 sts from cable needle
C3B = slip next st on to cable needle, hold at back of work, K2, then P1 from cable needle

BACK

Using 3¼mm needles and A, cast on 65 (73:81:89:97) sts. **1st rib row** K1, [P1, K1] to end. **2nd rib row** P1, [K1, P1] to end. With B, rep 1st and 2nd rows. With C, rep 1st and 2nd rows. With A, rep 1st and 2nd rows until work measures 6cm from beg, ending with 1st rib row **. **Next row** Rib 4(8:12:2:6), *M1, rib 2(2:2:3:3), rep from * to last 5(9:13:3:7) sts, M1, rib to end. 94(102:110:118:126) sts. Change to 4mm needles.

Commence pattern **1st row** (RS) P2(6: 2:6:2), [K6, P2] 2(2:3:3:4) times, [P2, C3B] twice, [C3F, P2] twice, P2, [K6, P2] twice, [P2, C3B] twice, [C3F, P2] twice, [P2, K6] 2(2:3:3:4) times, P2(6:2:6:2). **2nd row** K2(6:2:6:2), [P6, K2] 2(2:3:3:4) times, K2, P2, K3, P2, K2, P2, K3, P2, K4, [P6, K2] twice, K2, P2, K3, P2, K2, P2, K3, P2, K2, [K2, P6] 2(2:3:3:4) times, K2(6:2:6:2). **3rd row** P2(6:2:6:2), [K6, P2] 2(2:3:3:4) times, P1, [C3B, P2] twice, C3F, P2, C3F, P3, [K6, P2] twice, P1, [C3B, P2] twice, C3F, P2, C3F, P1, [P2, K6] 2(2:3:3:4) times, P2(6: 2:6:2). **4th row** K2(6:2:6:2), [P6, K2] 2(2:3:3:4) times, K1, P2, K3, P2, K4, P2, K3, P2, K3, [P6, K2] twice, K1, P2, K3, P2, K4, P2, K3, P2, K1, [K2, P6] 2(2:3:3:4) times, K2(6:2:6:2). **5th row** P2(6:2:6:2), [C6F, P2] 2(2:3:3:4) times, [C3B, P2] twice, [P2, C3F] twice, P2, [C6F, P2] twice, [C3B, P2] twice, [P2, C3F] twice, [P2,C6F] 2(2:3:3:4) times, P2(6:2:6:2). **6th row** K2(6:2:6:2), [P6, K2] 2(2:3:3:4) times, P2, K3, P2, K6, P2, K3, P2, K2, [P6, K2] twice, P2, K3, P2, K6, P2, K3, P2, [K2, P6] 2(2:3: 3:4) times, K2(6:2:6:2). **7th row** P2(6: 6:2), [K6, P2] 2(2:3:3:4) times, [C3F, P2] twice, [P2, C3B] twice, P2, [K6, P2] twice, [C3F, P2] twice, [P2, C3B] twice, [P2, K6] 2(2:3:3:4) times, P2(6:2:6:2). **8th row** As 4th. **9th row** P2(6:2:6:2), [K6, P2] 2(2:3:3: 4) times, P1, [C3F, P2] twice, C3B, P2, C3B, P3, [K6, P2] twice, P1, [C3F, P2] twice, C3B, P2, C3B, P1, [P2, K6] 2(2:3: 3:4) times, P2 (6:2:6:2). **10th row** As 2nd. **11th row** P2 (6:2:6:2), [K6, P2] 2(2:3:3:4) times, [P2, C3F] twice, [C3B, P2] twice, P2, [K6, P2] twice, [P2, C3F] twice, [C3B, P2] twice, [P2, K6] 2(2:3:3:4) times, P2(6:2: 6:2). **12th row** K2(6:2:6:2), [P6, K2] 2(2:3: 3:4) times, K3, P2, K3, P4, K3, P2, K5, [P6, K2] twice, K3, P2, K3, P4, K3, P2, K3, [K2, P6] 2(2:3:3: 4) times, K2(6:2:6:2). These 12 rows form the patt. Cont in patt until work measures 36(40:44:48:52)cm, ending with WS row.

Shape shoulders Cast off 31(34:37:40: 43) sts at beg of next 2 rows. Leave rem 32(34:36:38:40) sts on a holder.

FRONT

Work as given for back until front measures 21(24:27:30:33)cm from beg, ending WS row.

Divide for neck **Next row** Patt 47(51: 55:59:63), turn and leave rem sts on a spare needle. Complete left side of neck first. Keeping patt correct, dec one st at neck edge on next and every foll alt row until 31(34:37:40:43) sts rem. Cont without shaping until front matches back to shoulder, ending at a side edge. Cast off. With RS facing, rejoin A to rem sts, patt to end. Complete to match other side of neck.

SLEEVES

Using 3¼mm needles and A, cast on 31 (37:43:49:55) sts. Work as given for back from ** to **. **Next row** Rib 5(8:1:4:7), *M1, rib 1(1:2:2:2), rep from * to last 6(9: 2:5:8) sts, M1, rib to end. 52(58:64:70:76) sts. Change to 4mm needles.

Commence pattern **1st row** (RS) K0 (1:4:0:2), P0(2:2:1:2), [K6, P2] 2(2:2: 3:3) times, [P2, C3B] twice, [C3F, P2] twice, [P2, K6] 2(2:2:3:3) times, P0(2:2:1:2), K0 (1:4:0:2). **2nd row** P0(1:4:0:2), K0(2:2: 1:2), [P6, K2] 2(2:2:3:3) times, K2, P2, K3, P2, K2, P2, K3, P2, K2, [K2, P6] 2(2:2:3:3) times, K0(2:2:1:2), P0(1:4:0:2). **3rd row** K0(1:4:0:2), P0(2:2:1:2), [K6, P2] 2(2:2: 3:3) times, P1, [C3B, P2] twice, C3F, P2, C3F, P1, [P2, K6] 2(2:2:3:3) times, P0(2:2: 1:2), K0(1:4:0:2). **4th row** P0(1:4:0:2), K0 (2:2:1:2), [P6, K2] 2(2:2:3:3) times, K1, P2, K3, P2, K4, P2, K3, P2, K1, [K2, P6] 2(2:2: 3:3) times, K0(2:2:1:2), P0(1:4:0:2). These 4 rows set the patt. Cont in patt, inc one st at each end of next and every foll 3rd(3rd: 4th: 4th:5th) row, taking inc sts into the cable patt, until there are 88(94:100:106: 112) sts. Cont without shaping until sleeve measures 26(29:32:35:38)cm from beg, ending with a WS row. Cast off in patt.

NECKBAND

Join right shoulder seam. Using 3¼mm needles, A and with RS facing, K up 40(44: 48:52:56) sts down left front neck, M1 at centre front neck and mark this st, K up 40(44:48:52:56) sts up right front neck and K across 32(34:36:38:40) back neck sts. 113(123:133:143:153) sts. Beg with a 2nd row, work in rib as given for back in stripe sequence of 3 rows A, 2 rows C, 2 rows B, 2 rows A, at the same time, dec one st at each side of marked st at centre front on every row (note that centre front stitch is worked as K on RS and P on WS). Using A, cast off in rib, dec as before.

TO MAKE UP

Press according to directions on ball band. Join left shoulder and neckband seam. Place markers 15(16:17:18:19)cm down from shoulders on back and front. Sew in sleeves between markers. Join side and sleeve seams.

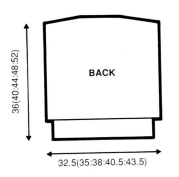

BACK

36(40:44:48:52)

32.5(35:38:40.5:43.5)

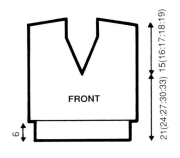

FRONT

21(24:27:30:33) 15(16:17:18:19)

6

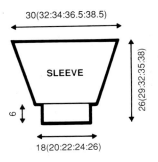

30(32:34:36.5:38.5)

SLEEVE

26(29:32:35:38)

6

18(20:22:24:26)

Bright Summer Sweater

A summer sweater with colourful sleeves and contrasting ribs.

Skill Rating Easy
Sizes To fit age 4(6:8) years
To fit chest 24(26:28)in/61(66:71)cm
Actual size 71(76:82)cm
Length to shoulder 36(41:46)cm *Sleeve seam* 25(29:33)cm
Materials 2(2:2) x 50g balls of 100% cotton Chunky in green (colour A),
3(4:5) balls same in navy (B) and 1(2:2) balls each in red (C) and yellow (D)
We used Tivoli Luxor
Pair each 4½mm and 5mm knitting needles • 8 buttons
Tension 18 sts and 25 rows to 10cm over st st on 5mm needles

BACK

Using 5mm needles and A, cast on 58(62: 68) sts. Work 10 rows K1, P1 rib. Change to B. Beg with a K row, st st 10 rows. Cast on 3 sts at beg of next 2 rows for top of side slits. 64(68:74) sts. Cont in st st until back measures 19(22:25)cm from beg, ending with a P row.

Shape armholes Dec one st at each end of every K row until 48(52:56) sts rem. Cont straight until back measures 34(39: 44)cm from beg, ending with a P row.

Shape neck **Next row** K18(19:20), turn. Cont on these sts only for 1st side and leave rem sts on a spare needle. Cast off 4 sts at beg of next row and on the foll alt row. 10(11:12) sts.

Shape shoulder Cast off 3 sts at beg of next row and on the foll alt row. Work 1 row. Cast off rem 4(5:6) sts. With RS of work facing, sl centre 12(14:16) sts on to a holder, rejoin yarn to inner end of rem sts, K to end. P 1 row. Complete to match 1st side.

FRONT

Work as given for back until front measures 8 rows less than back to beg of shoulder shaping, ending with a P row.

Shape neck **Next row** K19(20:21), turn. Cont on these sts only for 1st side and leave rem sts on a spare needle. Cast off 3 sts at beg of next row and on the foll 2 alt rows. 10(11:12) sts. Work 2 rows straight, ending at armhole edge.

Shape shoulder Cast off 3 sts at beg of next row and on the foll alt row. Work 1 row. Cast off rem 4(5:6) sts. With RS of work facing, sl centre 10(12:14) sts on to a holder, rejoin yarn to inner end of rem sts, K to end. P 1 row. Cast off 3 sts at beg of next row and on the foll 2 alt rows. 10(11:12) sts. Work 2 rows straight, ending at armhole edge.

Shape shoulder Work as 1st side.

RIGHT SLEEVE

Using 5mm needles and A, cast on 34(36: 38) sts. Work 10 rows K1, P1 rib. Change to C. Cont in st st inc one st at each end of 3rd row and every foll 4th row until there are 58(64:70) sts. Cont straight until sleeve measures 25(29:33)cm from beg, ending with a P row.

Shape top Dec one st at each end of every K row until 42(48:52) sts rem. Cast off loosely.

LEFT SLEEVE

Using 5mm needles and A, cast on 34(36: 38) sts. Work 10 rows K1, P1 rib. Change to D. Cont in st st inc one st at each end of 3rd row and every foll 4th row until there are 58(64:70) sts. Cont straight until sleeve measures 25(29:33)cm from beg, ending with a P row.

Shape top Dec one st at each end of every K row until 42(48:52) sts rem. Cast off loosely.

SIDE SLIT BANDS

Make 2 Using 5mm needles and A, cast on 10 sts. Work 20 rows K1, P1 rib. Cast off in rib.

NECKBAND

Join right shoulder seam. With RS facing, 4½mm needles and A, K up 17 sts down left front neck, K across 10(12:14) sts at centre front, K up 17 sts up right front neck and 11 sts down right back neck, K across 12(14:16) sts at centre back then K up 11 sts up left back neck. 78(82:86) sts. Work 10 rows K1, P1 rib. Cast off loosely in rib.

TO MAKE UP

Join left shoulder and neckband seam. Join side seams to top of side slits. Join sleeve seams. Set in sleeves. Sew side slit bands in place. Sew 3 buttons, evenly spaced, to each side slit band, and 1 button to centre of each cuff.

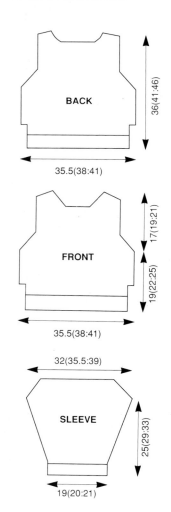

Winter Warmers

Our colourful and quick-to-knit hats, scarves and mitts will keep your little angel snug on the very coldest of winter days.

Skill Rating Medium
Sizes To fit age 3 to 7(8 to 12) years
Materials *1st colourway* (pink/jade): 7(8) x 50g balls of
100% wool Aran in pink (colour A) and 3 balls jade (B)
2nd colourway (yellow/blue): 6(7) balls same in yellow (C)
and 4(5) balls in blue (D)
3rd colourway (red/purple): 5(6) balls same
in each of red (E) and purple (F)
We used Sunbeam Aran Knit
Pair each 4mm and 5mm knitting needles
4mm crochet hook for scarf edging
Set each 4mm and 5mm double-pointed knitting needles for mitts
Tension 18 sts and 24 rows to 10cm over st st on 4mm needles

HAT

Using 4mm needles and B for 1st colourway, C for 2nd colourway or F for 3rd colourway, cast on 115(127) sts. **1st rib row** (RS) K1, [P1, K1] to end. **2nd rib row** (WS) P1, [K1, P1] to end. Rep these 2 rows 19 times more, then work 1st row again. **Dec row** (WS) P1(7), * P2tog, P2, rep from * to last 2(8) sts, P2 tog, P0(6). 86(98) sts. Change to 5mm needles. *For 1st colourway* change to A, *for 2nd colourway* cont with C and, for both, beg K row, work 20 rows st st. *For 3rd colourway* use separate ball of yarn for each panel **Next row** K15 (17)F, [14(16)E, 14(16)F] twice, 15(17)E. Cont as set and beg P, work 19 more rows.
Shape crown For all colourways **Dec row** (RS) K1, [skpo, K10(12), K2tog] 6 times, K1. 74(86) sts. Work 3 rows. **Dec row** K1, [skpo, K8(10), K2tog] 6 times, K1. P 1 row. **Dec row** K1, [skpo, K6(8), K2tog] 6 times, K1. P 1 row. Cont dec in this way, working 2 sts less between decs on next and every foll alt row until 14 sts rem. P 1 row. **Next row** K1, [K2 tog] to last st, K1. Break off yarn, thread yarn end through rem sts, draw up and secure.

TO MAKE UP

Join centre back seam, reversing seam at rib. Roll up the brim.

SCARF

Using 5mm needles and A for 1st colourway cast on 60(68) sts. *For 2nd and 3rd colourways* cast on 30(34) sts with C or E and 30(34) sts with D or F and cont with colours as set, twisting yarns on wrong side when changing colour to avoid making a hole. For all colourways beg K, row, cont in st st until work measures 120(132)cm. Cast off using matching colours.

TO MAKE UP

Join side edges. Fold scarf with seam at side edge for 1st and 2nd colourway or at centre for 3rd colourway. Matching colours, work a row of double crochet along each end to close openings.

MITTS

RIGHT MITT

Using a 4mm double-pointed needle and B for 1st colourway, C for 2nd colourway or E for 3rd colourway, cast on 28(32) sts. Divide sts between 3 needles, join in a round and mark start of each round by running a contrast thread up through work. **Rib round** [K1, P1] to end. Rep rib round 13(14) more times. Change to 5mm needles. For 2nd colourway, change to D. For all colourways work 9(11) rounds st st, (every round K) *.
Shape thumb **Next round** Sl first 4 sts onto a holder, turn and cast on 4 sts in their place, turn and K to end of round. ** Cont in st st until work measures 16(17.5)cm from beg, ending at contrast thread marker.

Shape top **Dec round** [Skpo, K10(12), K2tog] twice. **Dec round** [Skpo, K8(10), K2tog] twice. **Dec round** [Skpo, K6(8), K2 tog] twice. **Dec round** [Skpo, K4(6), K2 tog] twice. Place first 6(8) sts on one needle and rem 6(8) sts on another, graft the 2 sets of sts together.
Thumb Using B for 1st colourway, C for 2nd colourway or F for 3rd colourway, sl 4 sts of thumb onto one needle, using 2nd and 3rd needles, pick up and K6 sts from those cast on at base of thumb. 10 sts. K7(10) rounds. **Next round** [K2tog] 5 times. Break yarn, run end through rem sts, draw up and fasten off.

LEFT MITT

Work as right mitt to *.
Shape thumb K14(16), sl next 4 sts onto a holder, turn and cast on 4 sts in their place, turn and K to end of round. Complete as right mitt from **.

TASSELS

Make between 24 and 30 tassels, each 5cm long, from remaining yarn, using colours as shown in picture. Sew 8 tassels to each end of scarf, 6 tassels to top of the hat and remaining tassels to sides or backs of mitts.

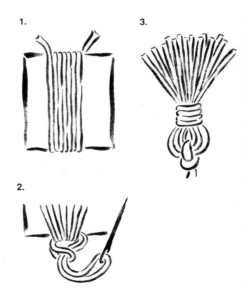

1. Wind yarn 7 times around 5cm square of card

2. Secure at one end by tying yarn around loops

3. Slide tassel off card. Bind yarn around tied end, cut loops at other end and trim.

Duffle Coat

This warm and cosy duffle coat with hood and front pockets uses only knit and purl stitches.

Skill Rating Medium
Sizes To fit age 4(6:8) years
To fit chest 24(26:28)in/61(66:71)cm
Actual size 80(84:90)cm
Length to shoulder 49(54:59)cm *Sleeve seam* 27(31:36)cm
Materials 6(7:7) x 100g balls of 100% wool Chunky in blue
We used Rowan Magpie
Pair each 5mm and 5½mm knitting needles
4mm crochet hook • 8 toggles • 2 small buttons
Tension 17 sts and 22 rows to 10cm over patt on 5½mm needles

BACK

Using 5mm needles cast on 67(71:75) sts. Beg K row, work 7 rows st st. **Next row** K to mark hemline. Change to 5½mm needles.

Commence pattern **1st row** (RS) K3, [P1, K3] to end. **2nd row** P. **3rd row** K1, [P1, K3] to last 2 sts, P1, K1. **4th row** P. These 4 rows form patt. Cont in patt until work measures 49(54:59)cm from hemline, ending with a WS row.

Shape shoulders Cast off 24(25:26) sts at beg of next 2 rows. Cast off rem 19(21:23) sts.

POCKET LINING

Make 2. Using 5½mm needles cast on 16 sts. Beg K row, work in st st for 10cm, ending with a P row. Leave sts on a spare needle.

LEFT FRONT

Using 5mm needles cast on 33(37:41) sts. K 1 row. Beg P row, cont in st st, inc one st at beg of 1st row and at this same edge on every row until there are 39(43:47) sts, ending with a K row. * **Next row** K. Change to 5½mm needles. Cont in patt as given for back until work measures 16(18:20)cm from hemline, ending with a WS row *.

Place pocket **Next row** Patt 8(8:9), sl next 16 sts onto a holder and in their place, patt across sts of one pocket lining, patt to end of row. Cont in patt until work measures 42(47:52)cm from hemline, ending with a RS row.

Shape neck Cast off 10 sts at beg of next row and 2 sts at beg of foll alt row. Dec one st at neck edge on every row until 24(25:26)sts rem. Cont straight until front matches back to shoulder, ending at side edge. Cast off.

RIGHT FRONT

Using 5mm needles cast on 33(37:41)sts K 1 row. Beg P row, cont in st st, inc one st at end of 1st row and at this same edge on every row until there are 39(43:47) sts, ending with a K row. Work as given for left front from * to *.

Place pocket **Next row** Patt 15(19:22), sl next 16 sts onto a holder and in their place, patt across sts of 2nd pocket lining, patt to end of row. Complete to match left front.

SLEEVES

Using 5mm needles cast on 35(35:39) sts. Beg K row, work 7 rows st st, ending with a K row. **Next row** K to mark hemline. Change to 5½mm needles and work in patt as given for back, inc one st at each end of 5th and every foll 4th row until there are 61(63:67) sts. Cont without shaping until sleeve measures 27(31: 36)cm from hemline, ending with a WS row. Cast off loosely.

HOOD

Using 5½mm needles cast on 7 sts. Work 2 rows in st st. Cont in patt as given for back, casting on 7 sts at beg of next row, 5 sts at beg of foll alt row, 3 sts at beg of foll alt row and 2 sts at beg of foll alt row. 24 sts. Inc one st at shaped edge on every foll 6th row until there are 29(31:33) sts. Work 5 rows without shaping. Dec one st at shaped edge on next and foll 2 alt rows, then dec one st at shaped edge on

next row, ending with a WS row. Cast off 5 sts at beg of next row and 4 sts at beg of foll alt row. Cast off rem sts. Work other side to match, reversing shapings.

Centre back panel Using 5½mm needles cast on 11 sts. Work in patt, inc one st at each end of 9th and every foll 8th row until there are 21 sts. Cont without shaping until work measures 36(42:48)cm, ending with a WS row. Cast off loosely. Join centre panel to two side panels, extending centre panel along top of side panels.

POCKET TOPS

Using 5mm needles and with RS facing, work 4 rows K1, P1 rib over each set of 16 sts on holders. Cast off in rib.

EDGINGS

Join shoulder seams. Using 5mm needles and with RS facing, K up 51(53:55) sts around neck edge. K 2 rows. Cast off.

Left front Using 5mm needles, with RS facing, K up 73(79:85) sts down front edge to hemline. Beg P row, work 2 rows st st. Dec one st at beg and at this same edge on every row until 68(74:80) sts rem. Cast off.

Right front Work to match left front edging, reversing shapings.

Hood Using 5mm needles and with RS facing, K up 94(102:110) sts around face edge of hood. Beg P row, work 7 rows st st. Cast off.

TO MAKE UP

Press according to directions on ball band. Place markers 17(18:19)cm down from shoulders on back and fronts. Sew in sleeves between markers. Fold back all edgings at hemlines and slip stitch in place, joining mitred edges. Join side and sleeve seams. Sew down pocket linings and ends of pocket tops. Sew on hood, beg and ending 5cm in from front edges.

Toggle fastenings With crochet hook, make a chain 42cm long. Fold in half and fasten loop 3cm from fold. Make 2 loops at other end. Work 3 more toggle fastenings, then sew them onto left front for a boy or right front for a girl. Make 4 chains each 16cm long and fasten each into a 'figure 8', then sew to other front to correspond. Make a buttonhole loop at corner of each front at neck edge. Sew one button on RS of one front and the other button on WS of other front to correspond with buttonhole loops. Sew on toggles.

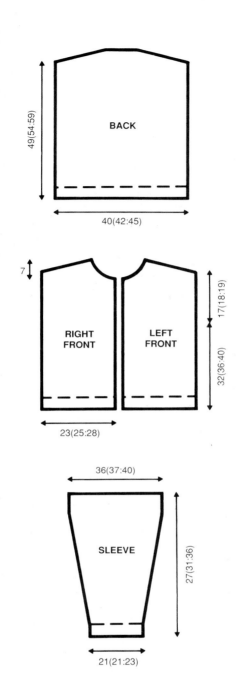

BACK

49(54:59)

40(42:45)

7

RIGHT
FRONT

LEFT
FRONT

17(18:19)

32(36:40)

23(25:28)

36(37:40)

SLEEVE

27(31:36)

21(21:23)

Traditional Fair Isle Sweater and Hat

A round-necked Fair Isle sweater with shoulder buttoning and matching hat, knitted in a beautiful traditional pattern.

Skill Rating Medium
Sizes Sweater: To fit age 2(4:6:8) years
To fit chest 22(24:26:28)in/56(61:66:71)cm
Actual size 64(68:73:78)cm
Length to shoulder 34(39:44:49)cm *Sleeve seam* 24(28:32:36)cm
Hat: Sizes correspond to sweater
Materials Sweater 3(3:3:4) x 50g balls of 45% acrylic/40%
Bri-Nylon/15% wool DK in fawn (colour A) and 1 ball same in
each of blue (B), rust (C), gold (D), cream (E) and olive (F)
Hat 1 ball each of 6 shades listed for sweater
We used Hayfield Grampian DK
Pair each of 3¼mm and 4mm knitting needles • 6 small buttons
Set each of 3¼mm and 4mm double-pointed knitting needles for hat
Tension 25 sts and 29 rows to 10cm over patt on 4mm needles

SWEATER

BACK

Using 3¼mm needles and A, cast on 69(75:81:87) sts. **1st rib row** (RS) K1 tbl, [P1, K1 tbl] to end. **2nd rib row** P1, [K1 tbl, P1] to end. Rep these 2 rows for 6cm, ending with a 1st rib row. **Inc row** Rib 2(5:4:7), [inc in next st, rib 6(6:7:7)] to last 4(7:5:8) sts, inc in next st, rib 3(6:4:7). 79(85:91:97) sts. Change to 4mm needles. Cont in st st from chart – see page 66. On 2-colour rows carry colour not in use loosely across WS. **1st row** (RS) Reading row 1 from right to left and beg at st indicated, K10(3:6:9), [work 20 patt sts] 3(4:4:4) times, K next 9(2:5:8) sts of chart. **2nd row** Reading row 2 from left to right and beg at st indicated, P9(2: 5:8), [work 20 patt sts] 3(4:4:4) times, P next 10(3:6:9) sts of chart.

Cont from chart in this way until back measures 32(37:42: 47)cm from beg, ending with a WS row.

Shape neck **Next row** Patt 29(31: 33:35), turn. Cont on these sts only for 1st side and leave rem sts on a spare needle. Keeping patt correct, dec one st at neck edge on next 3 rows. Cast off rem 26(28: 30:32) sts. With RS facing, sl centre 21(23:25:27) sts on to a holder, rejoin yarn to inner end of rem sts, patt to end. Complete to match 1st side.

FRONT

Work as back until front measures 10 rows less than back to shoulder, ending with a WS row.

Shape neck **Next row** Patt 30(32:34: 36), turn. Cont on these sts only for 1st side and leave rem sts on a spare needle. Dec one st at neck edge on next 4 rows. 26(28:30:32) sts. Patt 5 rows straight. Cast off. With RS facing, sl centre 19(21: 23:25) sts on to a holder, rejoin yarn to inner end of rem sts and patt to end. Complete to match the 1st side.

SLEEVES

Using 3¼mm needles and A, cast on 37 (39:41:43) sts. Rib 6cm as back, ending with a 1st rib row. **Inc row** Rib 1(2:3:4), [inc in next st, rib 2] to last 3(4:5:6) sts, inc in next st, rib 2(3:4:5). 49(51:53:55) sts. Change to 4mm needles. Cont in st st from chart. **1st row** (RS) Reading row 1 from right to left and beg at st indicated, K5(6:7:8), [work 20 patt sts] twice, K next 4(5:6:7) sts of chart. **2nd row** Reading row 2 from left to right and beg at st indicated, P4(5:6:7), [work 20 patt sts] twice, P next 5(6:7:8) sts of chart. Cont from chart inc one st at each end of 5th and every foll 4th(4th:5th:5th) row, taking inc sts into patt, until there are 71(75: 79:83) sts. Cont straight until the sleeve

measures 24(28:32:36)cm from beg, ending with a P row. Cast off loosely.

BACK NECKBAND

With RS facing, 3¼mm needles and A, K up 4 sts down right back neck, K across 21(23:25:27) sts on holder then K up 4 sts up left back neck. 29(31:33:35) sts. Beg with 2nd rib row, rib 5 rows. Cast off loosely in rib.

FRONT NECKBAND

With RS facing, 3¼mm needles and A, K up 10 sts down left front neck, K across 19(21:23:25) sts on holder, K up 10 sts up right front neck. 39(41:43:45) sts. Beg with 2nd rib row, rib 5 rows. Cast off loosely in rib.

BUTTONHOLE BANDS

With RS facing, 3¼mm needles and A, K up 29(31:33:35) sts across left front shoulder including ends of neckband. Beg with 2nd rib row, rib 3 rows as at beg of back. **Buttonhole row** (RS) Rib 4, [K2 tog, yo, rib 8(9:10:11)] twice, K2 tog, yo, rib 3. Rib 2 rows. Cast off in rib. Work right front buttonhole band to match, but beg buttonhole row rib 3 and end rib 4.

BUTTON BANDS

Work to match buttonhole bands but omit buttonholes.

TO MAKE UP

Lap buttonhole bands over button bands and join ends at armhole edges. Mark position of underarms 14(15:16:17)cm down from centre of buttonhole band on back and front. Sew on sleeves between markers. Join side and sleeve seams. Sew on buttons.

HAT

Using set of 3¼mm double-pointed needles and A, cast on 90(100:110:120) sts. Mark last st with a coloured thread to show end of round. **1st rib round** [K1 tbl, P1] to end. **2nd rib round** [K1, P1 tbl] to end. Rep these 2 rounds twice, then work 1st rib round again. **Inc round** *1st size only* * [Inc in next st, rib 1] 4 times, inc in next st, rep from * to end. 140 sts. *2nd size only* [Inc in each of next 2 sts, rib 1, inc in next st, rib 1] to end. 160 sts. *3rd size only* * [Inc in next st, rib 1, inc in each of next 2 sts, rib 1] twice,

inc in next st, rep from * to end. 180 sts.
4th size only [Inc in each of next 2 sts, rib 1] to end. 200 sts. *All sizes* Change to set of 4mm double-pointed needles. Work throughout in st st (every round K). Work 0(0:0:2) rounds. Cont in patt reading chart from right to left for every round and working 20 patt sts 7(8:9:10) times on every round. Work rounds 5 to 17 (3 to 17:1 to 17:1 to 17), then work rounds 3 to 13. **Dec round** With A, [K6, K3 tog, K1, K3 tog, K7] to end. 112(128: 144:160) sts. K 1 round A. **Next round** [1A, 1C] to end. **Next round** [1C, 1A] to end. Work 2 rounds A.

Shape crown **1st round** * [1A, 1C] 3 times, K3 tog A, 1C, [1A, 1C] 3 times, rep from * to end. 98(112:126:140) sts. **2nd round** [1C, 1A] to end. **3rd round** With A, [K5, K3 tog, K6] to end. **4th round** With A, [K4, K3 tog, K5) to end. **5th round** * 1C, 1A, 1C, K3 tog A, [1C, 1A] twice, rep from * to end. **6th round** [1A, 1C, K3 tog A, 1C, 1A, 1C] to end. **7th round** With A, [K1, K3 tog, K2] to end. **8th round** With A, [K3 tog, K1] to end. 14(16:18:20) sts. Cut yarn leaving approx 20 cm. Thread end through rem sts, draw up and secure.

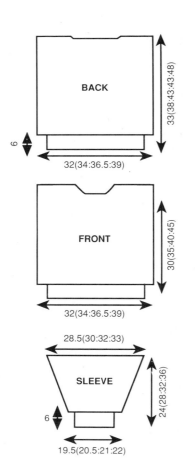

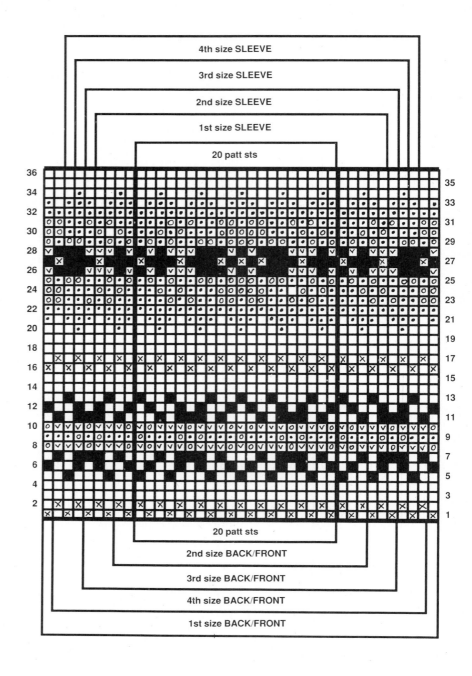

	A		D
□	A	○	D
●	B	V	E
X	C	■	F

66 / CLASSIC KNITS

patterned
KNITS

Pierrot Sweater and Cropped Pants

A motif knitted sweater with frilled edge and easy to knit short pantaloons.

Skill Rating Medium
Sizes To fit age 6(12:24) months
Sweater: To fit chest 18(20:22)in/46(51:56)cm
Actual size 56(60:63)cm
Length to shoulder with frill 31(34:37)cm *Sleeve seam* 22(23:24)cm
Pants: Length with cuff turned back 30(32:34)cm
Materials Sweater 3(4:5) x 50g balls of 55% wool/25% acrylic/20%
nylon 4 ply in yellow (colour A) and 1 ball same in black (B)
Pants 2(3:3) balls same in black (B) and 1 ball same in yellow (A)
We used Patons Diploma Gold 4 ply
Pair each 2¾mm and 3¼mm knitting needles
Waist length of narrow elastic for pants
Tension 28 sts and 36 rows to 10cm over st st on 3¼mm needles

SWEATER

BACK

Using 3¼mm needles and A, cast on 130(134:138) sts. Beg with a K row, work 10 rows st st, ending with a WS row. **Next row** K0(1:7), * K3(4:3), sl 1, K1, psso, rep from * to last 0(1:11) sts, K to end. 104(112:114) sts. Work 3 rows st st. **Next row** K0(0:4), * K2, sl 1, K1, psso, rep from * to last 0(0:6) sts, K 0(0:6). 78(84:88) sts. P 1 row. Change to 2¾mm needles. **1st and every row** [K1, P1] to end. Rep this row 9 more times. Change to 3¼mm needles. Work in patt from complete chart beg at size indicated, reading odd-numbered (K) rows from right to left and even-numbered (P) rows from left to right. Use a separate ball for each motif and twist yarns together when changing colour to avoid a hole. Cont until row 88(100:110) has been worked

Shape shoulders Cast off 20(22:23) sts, K38(40:42) sts, cast off rem 20(22:23) sts. Leave rem 38(40:42) sts on a holder.

FRONT

Work as given for back until row 72 (84:92) of chart has been completed.

Shape neck Work from chart as folls: **Next row** Patt 28(30:32), turn and leave rem sts on a spare needle. Dec one st at neck edge on next and every alt row until 20(22:23) sts rem, ending with a WS row. Cast off. With RS facing sl centre 22(24:24) sts on to a holder, rejoin yarn to rem sts and patt to end. Complete to match other side.

SLEEVES

Using 2¾mm needles and B, cast on 42(44:46) sts. Work 3cm in K1, P1 rib as given for back, ending with a RS row. **Next row** Rib 3(4:1), * M1, rib 5(4:4), rep from * to last 4(4:1) sts, M1, rib to end. 50(54:58) sts. Change to 3¼mm needles. Beg as indicated for sleeves, work in patt from chart, inc one st at each end of 5th and every foll 4th row until there are 78(82:88) sts. Work 11(15:15) rows straight. Cast off.

NECKBAND

Join right shoulder seam. Using 2¾mm needles, A and with RS facing, K up 19 sts down left front neck, K across 22(24:24) sts of centre front neck, K up 19 sts up right front neck and K across 38(40:42) sts of back neck. 98(102:104) sts. Work 4cm K1, P1 rib. Cast off in rib.

TO MAKE UP

Press according to directions on ball band. Join left shoulder and neckband seam. Place markers 14(15:16)cm down from shoulders on back and front. Sew sleeves between markers. Join side and sleeve seams. Fold neckband in half on to WS, slip stitch in place.

PANTS

BACK

Right leg Using 2¾mm needles and A, cast on 40(40:42) sts and work 8cm K1, P1 rib, ending with a RS row. **Next row** Rib 2(6:3), * M1, rib 3(2:3), rep from * to last 2(6:3) sts, M1, rib to end. 53(55:55) sts. Change to 3¼mm needles. Using B, beg K row, work 8cm st st, ending with a WS row **. **Next row** K to end, turn and cast off 3 sts, sl rem 50(52:52) sts onto a spare needle.

Left leg Work as given for right leg to **. **Next row** Cast off 3 sts, K to end. 50(52:52) sts.

Join legs **Next row** P across 50(52:52) sts of left leg, then P across 50(52:52) sts of right leg. 100(104:104) sts. **Next row** K1(3:3), * sl 1, K1, psso, K3, rep from * to last 4(6:6) sts, sl 1, K1, psso, K to end. 80(84:84) sts. Beg P row, cont in st st until work measures 32(34:36)cm from beg, ending with a WS row. Change to 2¾mm needles and work 4cm in K1, P1 rib. Cast off in rib.

FRONT

Work as given for back.

TO MAKE UP

Press according to directions on ball band. Join inside leg and front seams. Fold waist rib in half to WS. Leaving an opening for elastic, slip stitch in place. Thread elastic through and join ends. Join opening. Turn up cuffs.

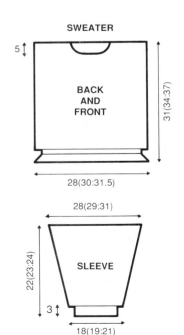

SWEATER

5

BACK AND FRONT

31(34:37)

28(30:31.5)

28(29:31)

22(23:24)

SLEEVE

3

18(19:21)

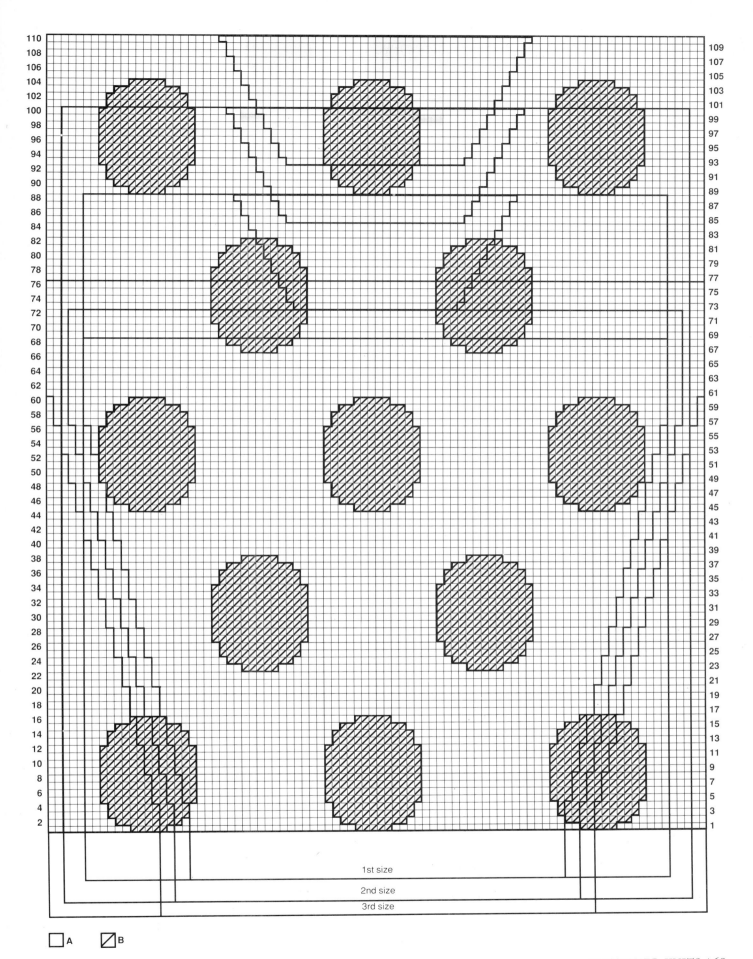

1st size

2nd size

3rd size

A   B

Scottie Dog Sweater and Beret

The Scottie dog borders will make this Aran sweater and beret set every little girl's best friend.

Skill Rating Medium
Sizes Sweater: To fit age 2(4:6:8:10) years
To fit chest 22(24:26:28:30)in/56(61:66:71:76)cm
Actual size 64(70:76:82:88)cm
Length to shoulder 37(40:42:47:52)cm *Sleeve seam* 26(29:31:34:37)cm
Beret: To fit 2-4(6-10) years
Materials Sweater and Beret 2(3:3:3:3) x 100g balls of 100% acrylic Aran
in red (colour A) and 1 ball in navy (B)
We used Littlewoods Economy Aran
Pair each of 4mm and 5mm knitting needles
Pair each of 4mm and 5mm double-pointed knitting needles for beret
Tension 17 sts and 23 rows to 10cm over st st on 5mm needles

SWEATER

BACK

Using 4mm needles and B, cast on 54(58:66:70:74) sts. Work striped rib carrying colour not in use loosely across back (WS) on 1st row and on same side on every foll row: **Rib row** [K1B, P1B, K1A, P1A] to last 2 sts, K1B, P1B. Rep rib row 9 times, inc one st at end of the last row on 2nd and 5th sizes only and dec one st at end of last row on 3rd size only. 54(59:65: 70:75) sts. Change to 5mm needles. With A, K1 row and P1 row. Cont in st st from chart 1, carrying colour not in use loosely across WS. **1st row** (RS) Reading row 1 of chart 1 from right to left, K 1st 0(1:0:0:1) st, rep 4 patt sts to last 2(2:1:2:2) sts, K next 2(2:1:2:2) sts of chart. **2nd row** Reading row 2 of chart 1 from left to right, P2(2:1:2:2) sts of chart, rep 4 patt sts to last 0(1:0:0:1) st, P last 0(1:0:0:1) st of chart. **3rd row** As 1st row but working row 3 of chart. With A, P1 row, K1 row and P1 row. Cont in st st from chart 2. **1st row** (RS) K2(3:1:1:2)A, * reading chart from right to left, K11 sts of row 1, K2(3:2:3:4)A, rep from * 2(2: 3:3:3) times, K11 sts of chart, K2(3:1: 2:2)A. **2nd row** P2(3:1:2:2)A, * reading chart from left to right, P11 sts of row 2, P2(3:2:3:4)A, rep from * 2(2:3:3:3) times, P11 sts of chart, P2(3:1:1:2)A. Cont until row 12 has been worked. Cont in A until back measures 37(40:42:47:52)cm from beg, ending with a P row.
Shape shoulders Cast off 9(10:11:12:

13) sts at beg of next 4 rows. Leave rem 18(19:21:22:23) sts on a holder.

FRONT

Work as back until front measures 12 rows less than back to beg of shoulder shaping, ending with a P row.
Shape neck **Next row** K24(26:28: 30:32), turn. Cont on these sts only for 1st side and leave rem sts on a spare needle. Dec one st at neck edge on next 6 rows. 18(20:22:24:26) sts. Work 5 rows straight, ending at side edge.
Shape shoulder Cast off 9(10:11: 12:13) sts at beg of next row. Work 1 row. Cast off rem 9(10:11:12:13) sts. With RS facing, sl the centre 6(7:9:10:11) sts on to a holder, rejoin A to inner end of sts on spare needle and K to end. Complete to match 1st side, working 1 extra row straight before shaping shoulder.

SLEEVES

Using 4mm needles and B, cast on 34(34:36:36:38) sts. Break off B; join A. Work 11 rows in K1, P1 rib. **Inc row** Rib 4(4:2:2:3), [inc in next st, rib 4(4:5:5:5)] to last 5(5:4:4:5) sts, inc in next st, rib 4(4:3:3:4). 40(40:42:42:44) sts. Change to 5mm needles. Cont in st st, inc one st at each end of 3rd row and every foll 8th(8th:8th:7th:6th) row until there are 50(50:54:58:62) sts. Cont straight until sleeve measures 26(29: 31:34:37)cm from beg, ending with a P row. Cast off loosely.

NECKBAND

Join right shoulder seam. With RS facing, using 5mm needles and B, K up 15 sts down left front neck, inc one st at centre on 2nd, 3rd and 5th sizes only, K across 6(7:9:10:11) sts on front holder, K up 15 sts up right front neck, inc one st at centre on 2nd, 3rd and 5th sizes only, K across 18(19:21:22:23) sts on back holder. 54(58:62:62:66) sts. Rib 3 rows as at beg of back. With B, cast off loosely in rib.

TO MAKE UP

Join left shoulder and neckband seam. Mark position of underarms 15(15: 16:17:18)cm down from shoulders on back and front. Sew on sleeves between the markers. Join side and sleeve seams.

BERET

Using set of 4mm double-pointed needles and B, cast on 88(92) sts evenly over 3 needles. **Rib round** Carrying colour not in use loosely across WS, [K1B, P1B, K1A, P1A] to end. Mark last st of round with a contrast thread. Rep rib round 6 times. Break off B. **Inc round** [K1, M1, K1] to end. 132(138) sts. Change to 5mm double-pointed needles. K 9 rounds. **Inc round** [K33(23), M1] 4(6) times. 136(144) sts. K 3 rounds.
Shape crown **1st round** [K15(16), K2 tog] 8 times. **2nd and every alt round** K. **3rd round** [K14(15), K2 tog] 8 times. **5th round** [K13(14), K2 tog] 8 times. Cont in this way, working 1 fewer st before the K2 tog on every alt round until 16 sts rem. **Last round** [K2 tog] 8 times. Break off yarn, thread end through rem sts, draw up and secure. Make a pompom with B and sew to top.

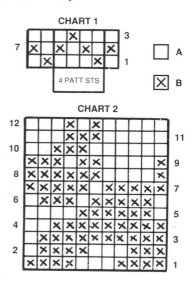

CHART 1

4 PATT STS

☐ A

☒ B

CHART 2

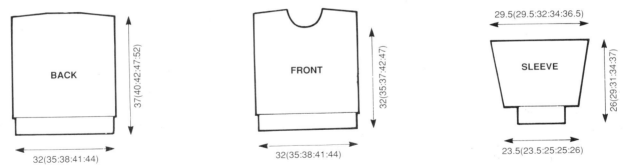

BACK

37(40:42:47:52)

32(35:38:41:44)

FRONT

32(35:37:42:47)

32(35:38:41:44)

29.5(29.5:32:34:36.5)

SLEEVE

26(29:31:34:37)

23.5(23.5:25:25:26)

Geometric Cardigan

This cosy cardigan knitted in five colours is guaranteed to brighten up the dullest day.

Skill Rating Experienced
Sizes To fit age 4(6:8) years
To fit chest 24(26:28)in/61(66:71)cm
Actual size 70(78.5:88)cm
Length 38(43:47.5)cm *Sleeve seam* 31.5(36:41)cm
Materials 2(2:3) x 50g balls of 50% Courtelle/40% Bri-Nylon/10% wool DK
in cream (colour A), 1(2:2) balls same in red (B) and blue (C),
1 ball each in jade (D) and amber (E)
We used Wendy Family Choice DK
Pair each of 3¼mm and 4mm knitting needles • 7 buttons
Tension 25 sts and 26 rows to 10cm over patt on 4mm needles

BACK

Using 3¼mm needles and A, cast on 67 (77:87) sts. **1st rib row** (RS) K1, [P1, K1] to end. **2nd rib row** P1, [K1, P1] to end. Rep these 2 rows 8 times, then work 1st rib row again. **Next row** Rib 1(2:3), [inc in next st, rib 3] to last 2(3:4) sts, inc in next st, rib 1(2:3). 84(96:108) sts. Change to 4mm needles and cont in st st from chart. Read odd-numbered (K) rows from right to left and even-numbered (P) rows from left to right. Weave colours not in use loosely across WS of work. **1st row** (RS) K sts 1 to 24(7 to 24:1 to 24), [K sts 1 to 24] 2(3:3) times, K sts 1 to 12(1 to 6:1 to 12). **2nd row** P sts 12 to 1(6 to 1:12 to 1), [P sts 24 to 1] 2(3:3) times, P sts 24 to 1(24 to 7:24 to 1). Cont in patt as set until 24 rows of chart have been worked. Rep these 24 rows until a total of 80(92:104) chart rows have been completed, thus ending with an 8th(20th:8th) row.
Shape neck **Next row** Patt 32(38:44), cast off next 20 sts, patt to end. Cont on last set of 32(38:44) sts and leave rem sts on a spare needle. Patt 1 row. Cast off 4(5: 6) sts at beg of next row. Patt 1 row. Cast off rem 28(33:38) sts. With WS facing, rejoin yarn to inner end of sts on spare needle and complete to match other side of neck.

RIGHT FRONT

Using 3¼mm needles and A, cast on 41 (47:51) sts. Rib 4 rows as given for back.
1st buttonhole row (RS) Rib 4, cast off 2, rib to end. **2nd buttonhole row** Rib to last 4 sts, cast on 2, rib 4. Rib 10 rows. Rep 1st and 2nd buttonhole rows. Rib 1 row. **Next row** Rib 4(3:1), [inc in next st, rib

2(3:3)] to last 13(12:10) sts, inc in next st, rib 4(3:1), turn and leave rem 8 sts on a safety pin for buttonhole band. Change to 4mm needles and cont from chart on these 42(48:54) sts. **1st row** (RS) Beg with st 7(7:19), end with st 24(6:24). **2nd row** Beg with st 24(6:24), end with st 7(7:19). Cont in patt as set until 72(84:96) chart rows have been worked, ending with a 24th(12th:24th) row.
Shape neck Cast off 8(9:10) sts at beg of next row. Patt 1 row. Dec one st at neck edge on next 6 rows. 28(33:38) sts. Patt straight until front matches back to shoulder. Cast off.

LEFT FRONT

Using 3¼mm needles and A, cast on 41 (47:51) sts. Rib 19 rows as given for back. **Next row** Rib 8 and leave on safety pin, rib 4(3:1), [inc in next st, rib 2(3:3)] to last 5(4:2) sts, inc in next st, rib 4(3:1). Change to 4mm needles and cont from chart on these 42(48:54) sts. **1st row** (RS) Beg with st 13(7:13), end with st 6(6:18). **2nd row** Beg with st 6(6:18), end with st 13(7:13). Complete to match right front ending with a 23rd (11th: 23rd) row of chart before shaping neck.

SLEEVES

Using 3¼mm needles and A, cast on 43 (47:49)sts. Rib 11 rows as given for back. **Next row** Rib 3(2:3), [inc in next st, rib 2] to last 1(0:1) st, rib 1(0:1). 56(62:64) sts. Change to 4mm needles and cont from chart. **1st row** (RS) Beg with st 3(24:23), end with st 10(13:14). **2nd row** Beg with st 10(13:14), end with st 3(24:23). Cont in patt, at the same time inc one st at each end of next row and every foll 4th(4th:5th) row, taking inc sts into patt, until there are 90(100:102) sts. Patt straight until a total of 72(84:96) chart rows have been completed, ending with a 24th(12th:24th) row. Cast off loosely.

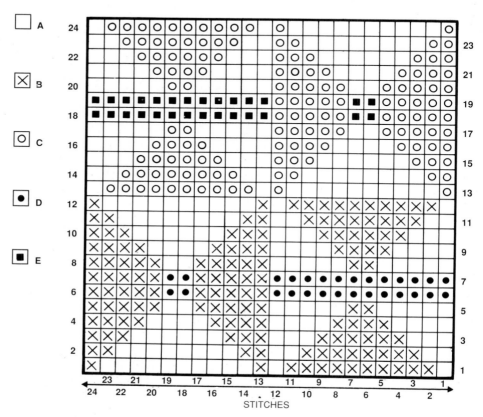

STITCHES

BUTTON BAND

With RS facing and 3¼mm needles, rejoin A to sts on safety pin. Rib as set until band, when slightly stretched, will fit up left front to beg of neck shaping, ending WS row. Leave sts on safety pin. Sew in place. Mark positions for 7 buttons, the 1st and 2nd to correspond to buttonholes in right front; the 7th, 1.5cm below top edge and the rem 4 spaced evenly between.

BUTTONHOLE BAND

With WS facing and 3¼mm needles, rejoin A to sts on safety pin. Work as for button band, working buttonholes as before to match markers. Leave sts on safety pin. Sew in place.

COLLAR

Join shoulder seams. With RS of work facing, 3¼mm needles and A, rib across 8 sts on safety pin, K up 18(19:20) sts up right front neck, 27(29:31) sts around back neck and 18(19:20) sts down left front neck, rib across 8 sts on safety pin. 79(83:87) sts. **Next row** P1, [K1, P1] 5(6:7) times, * in next st work K1, P1 and K1, [P1, K1] twice, in next st work P1, K1 and P1, [K1, P1] twice, rep from * 5 times, [K1, P1] 4(5:6) times. 103(107:111) sts. Cont in rib until collar measures 7cm. Cast off loosely in rib.

TO MAKE UP

Place markers 18(20:20.5)cm down from the shoulders on back and fronts. Sew in sleeves between markers. Join side and sleeve seams. Sew on buttons.

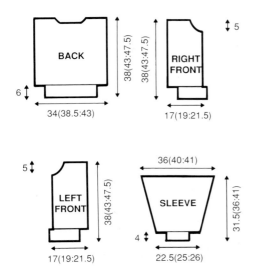

Colourful Cardigan

A traditional Fair Isle pattern is given a new look when knitted in bright colours. The bands are worked using a two colour rib.

Skill Rating Medium
Sizes To fit age 6 months(1:2:4:6) years
To fit chest 18(20:22:24:26)in/46(51:56:61:66)cm
Actual size 56(61:66:71:76)cm
Length to shoulder 23(28:32:38:42)cm *Sleeve seam* 17(21:24:28:32)cm
Materials 2(2:2:2:3) x 50g balls of 100% cotton DK in yellow (colour A), 2(2:2:3:3) balls same in cerise (B) and 1 ball each of same in blue (C) and green (D)
We used Sunbeam Cotton Classic DK
Pair each of 3¼mm and 4½mm needles
4(4:5:5:6) buttons
Tension 24 sts and 24 rows to 10cm over Fair Isle on 4½mm needles

BACK

Using 3¼mm needles and A, cast on 62 (66:70:78:82) sts. Work in 2-colour rib carrying colour not in use loosely across WS: **1st row** (RS) K2B, [K2A, K2B] to end. **2nd row** P2B, [K2A, P2B] to end. Rep these 2 rows for 3(4:4:4:5)cm, ending with a 1st row. Cut off A. **Next row** P6(5:6:5:4), * inc in next st, P11(8:6:10:8), rep from * to last 8(7:8:7:6) sts, inc in next st, P7(6:7: 6:5). 67(73:79:85:91) sts. Change to 4½mm needles. Cont in st st from chart, stranding colours not in use loosely across WS: *1st, 3rd and 5th sizes only* **1st row** K with B. **2nd row** Reading 2nd row of chart from left to right, P sts 4 to 1, [P sts 12 to 1] to last 3 sts, P sts 12 to 10. **3rd row** Reading 3rd row of chart from right to left, K sts 10 to 12, [K sts 1 to 12] to last 4 sts, K sts 1 to 4. *2nd and 4th sizes only* **1st row** K with B. **2nd row** Reading 2nd row of chart from left to right, P st 1, [P sts 12 to 1] to end. **3rd row** Reading 3rd row of chart from right to left, [K sts 1 to 12] to last st, K st 1. *All sizes* Cont from chart as set until all 20 rows have been completed. Rep these 20 rows until work measures 23(28:32:38:42)cm from beg, ending with a WS row.
Shape shoulders Cast off 12(13:14:15: 16) sts at beg of next 2 rows and 11(12:13: 14:15) sts at beg of foll 2 rows. Leave rem 21(23:25: 27:29) sts on a holder.

LEFT FRONT

Using 3¼mm needles and A, cast on 30 (30:34:38:38) sts. Work rib as back, ending with a 1st row. Cut off A. **Next row** P7 (2:4:5:3), * inc in next st, P14(5:7:12:5), rep from * 0(3:2:1:4) times, inc in next

st, P7(3:5:6:4). 32(35:38:41:44) sts. Change to 4½mm needles. Cont from chart reading odd-numbered (K) rows from right to left and even-numbered (P) rows from left to right, as before. Beg RS rows with st 10(1:10:1:10), end with st 5(11:11:5:5). Beg WS rows with st 5(11: 11:5:5), end with st 10(1:10:1:10). Cont in patt until front measures 12(16:19:24: 27)cm from beg, ending with a WS row.
Shape neck Dec one st at end of every K row until 23(25:27:29:31) sts rem. Patt straight until front matches back to shoulder, ending at side edge.
Shape shoulder Cast off 12(13:14:15: 16) sts at beg of next row. Patt 1 row. Cast off rem 11(12:13:14:15) sts.

RIGHT FRONT

Work to match left front, reversing all shapings and working the foll sts of chart: Beg RS rows with st 9(3:3:9:9), end with st 4(1:4:1:4). Beg WS rows with st 4(1:4:1:4), end with st 9(3:3:9:9).

SLEEVES

Using 3¼mm needles and A, cast on 30 (34:34:38:38) sts. Work rib as back, ending with a 1st row. Cut off A. **Next row** P2(2: 1:2:0), * inc in each of next 1(1:2: 2:3) sts, P1, rep from * to last 4(4:3:3:2) sts, inc in each of next 1(1:1:1:2) sts, P3(3:2:2:0). 43(49:55:61:67) sts. Change to 4½mm needles. Cont in patt as back, inc one st at each end of 3rd row and every foll 5th(6th: 8th:12th:16th) row, taking inc sts into patt, until there are 55(61:67: 71:75) sts. Patt straight until work measures 17(21:24: 28:32)cm from beg, ending with a WS row. Cast off loosely.

FRONT BAND

Join shoulder seams. With right side of work facing, 3¼mm needles and B, K up 34(44:52:64:72) sts up right front to beg of neck shaping and 34(37:40:43:46) sts to shoulder seam, K across sts at back neck inc one st at centre, K up 34(37:40:43:46) sts down left front to beg of neck shaping and 34(44:52:64:72) sts to lower edge. 158 (186:210:242:266) sts. Beg with 2nd row, cont in rib as at beg of back. Rib 1 row. **1st buttonhole row** (RS) Rib 2, * cast off next 2 sts, rib 7(10:9:12:11) including st rem on right needle after casting off, rep from * 2(2:3:3:4) times, cast off next 2 sts, rib to end. **2nd buttonhole row** Rib to end casting on 2 sts over each cast-off group of 1st row. Rib 2 rows. Cast off in rib.

TO MAKE UP

Place markers 11.5(13:14:15:16)cm down from shoulders on back and fronts. Sew in sleeves between markers. Join side and sleeve seams. Sew on buttons.

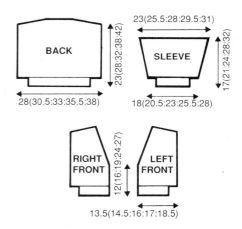

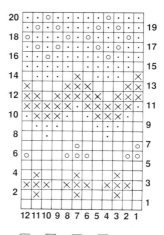

Zig Zag Fair Isle

Knitted in a simple all-over Fair Isle pattern, this child's sweater has zigzag borders and dropped shoulders.

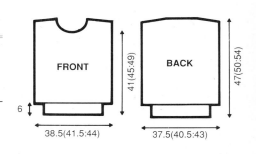

FRONT 41(45:49) 38.5(41.5:44) 6

BACK 47(50:54) 37.5(40.5:43)

Skill Rating Medium
Sizes To fit age 5-6(7-8:9-10) years
To fit chest 25-26(27-28:29-30)in/64-66(68-71:74-76)cm
Actual size 77(83:88)cm
Length to shoulder 47(50:54)cm *Sleeve seam* 35(38:40)cm
Materials 2(2:3) x 50g balls of 55% wool/25%acrylic/20% nylon DK in jade
(colour A), 1(1:2) balls in scarlet (B) and 5(5:6) balls in yellow (C)
We used Patons Diploma Gold DK
Pair each of 3¼mm and 4½mm knitting needles
Tension 22 sts and 24 rows to 10cm over patt on 4½mm needles

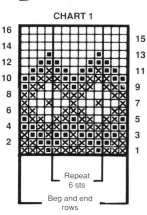

SLEEVE 38(40:42) 35(38:40) 5 22(22:25)

 A
 B
□ C

BACK

Using 3¼mm needles and A, cast on 82(90:94) sts. **1st rib row** (RS) K2, [P2, K2] to end. **2nd rib row** P2, [K2, P2] to end. Rep these 2 rows for 6cm, ending with a 2nd rib row and inc 3(1:3) sts evenly across last row. 85(91:97) sts. Change to 4½mm needles. Beg with a K row, cont in st st and patt 1st to 16th rows from chart 1, reading odd-numbered (K) rows from right to left and even-numbered (P) rows from left to right. Strand colours not in use loosely across WS of work. Now work from chart 2. Work 1st to 32nd rows 2(2:3) times, then work 1st to 18th(26th:4th) rows once more.

Shape shoulders Keeping patt correct, cast off 12(13:14) sts at beg of next 4 rows. Leave rem 37(39:41) sts on a spare needle.

FRONT

Work as given for back until front measures 14(12:12) rows less than back to shoulders, thus ending with a 4th (14th:24th) row of chart 2.

Shape neck **Next row** Patt 30(32:34) sts, turn. Cont on these sts only leaving rem sts on a spare needle. Dec 1 st at neck edge on every row until 24(26:28) sts rem. Patt 7(5:5) rows straight, thus front matches back to shoulder, ending at side edge.

Shape shoulder Cast off 12(13:14) sts at beg of next row. Patt 1 row. Cast off rem 12(13:14) sts. With RS of work facing, sl centre 25(27:29) sts onto a holder, rejoin yarn to inner end of rem sts and patt to end. Complete to match

other side, working 1 extra row straight before shaping shoulder.

SLEEVES

Using 3¼mm needles and A, cast on 46(46:50) sts. Rib 5cm as given for back, ending with a 2nd rib row and inc 3(3:5) sts evenly across last row. 49(49:55) sts. Change to 4½mm needles. Inc one st at each end of 3rd row and every foll 4th row and taking inc sts into patt, work 1st to 16th rows of chart 1 then rep 1st to 32nd rows of chart 2 until there are 83(87:93) sts. Patt 5(5:9) rows straight, thus ending with a 24th(32nd:4th) row of chart 2. Cast off loosely.

NECKBAND

Join right shoulder seam. With RS of work facing, using 3¼mm needles and C, K up 16 sts down left front neck, K across 25(27:29) sts at centre front, K up 16 sts up right front neck then K across 37(39:41) sts of back neck. 94(98:102) sts. Beg with 2nd rib row, rib 3cm as given for back. Cast off loosely in rib.

TO MAKE UP

Join left shoulder and neckband seam. Mark position of underarms 19(20:21) cm down from shoulders on back and front. Sew in sleeves between markers. Join side and sleeve seams.

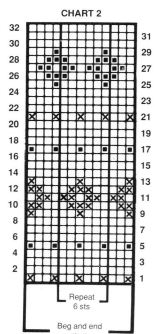

CHART 1
Repeat 6 sts
Beg and end rows

CHART 2
Repeat 6 sts
Beg and end rows

Teddy Bear Sweater

This simply-styled sweater is knitted in an easy wash yarn. Teddy motifs on front and sleeves are knitted in, with faces embroidered on afterwards.

Skill Rating Medium
Sizes To fit age 2(4:6) years
To fit chest 22(24:26)in/56(61:66)cm
Actual size 63(68:73)cm
Length to shoulder 39(42:45)cm *Sleeve seam* 29(31:34)cm
Materials 3(4:5) x 50g balls of 45% acrylic/40% Bri-Nylon/15% wool DK
in green (colour A) 1 ball same in each of gold (B) and red (C)
We used Sirdar Country Style DK
Pair each of 3¼mm and 4mm knitting needles
3¼mm circular knitting needle, 40cm long
Tension 24 sts and 30 rows to 10cm over st st on 4mm needles.

BACK

Using 3¼mm needles and A, cast on 62 (68:74) sts. **1st and every rib row** [K1, P1] to end. Rep this row for 5cm, ending with a RS row. **Next row** Rib 5(8:5), * M1, rib 4(4:5), rep from * to last 5(8:4) sts, M1, rib to end. 76(82:88) sts **. Change to 4mm needles. Beg with a K row, cont straight in st st until work measures 39(42:45)cm, ending with a WS row.

Shape shoulders Cast off 11(12:13) sts at beg of next 4 rows. Leave rem 32(34: 36) sts on a holder for back neck

FRONT

Work as given for back to **. Change to 4mm needles. Beg with a K row work 2 rows st st. Cont in patt from chart, reading odd-numbered (K) rows from right to left and even-numbered (P) rows from left to right. Use a separate ball of yarn for each area of colour and twist yarns together when changing colour to avoid a hole. Set chart as folls: **1st row** with A, K2(4:5) sts, [work 22 sts across 1st row of chart, with A, K3(4:6)] twice, work 22 sts across 1st row of chart, with A, K to end. Cont in patt as set until 34 rows have been completed. Cont in A until work measures 34(37:40)cm from beg, ending with a WS row.

Shape neck **Next row** K28(30:32) sts, turn and cont on these sts only for left side of neck, leave rem sts on a spare needle. Dec one st at neck edge on every row until 22(24:26) sts rem. Cont without shaping until front measures same as back to shoulder, ending at side edge.

Shape shoulder Cast off 11(12:13) sts at beg of next row. Work 1 row. Cast off rem 11(12:13) sts. With RS of work facing, sl first 10(11:12) sts from spare needle onto a holder, place a marker, sl next 10(11:12) sts onto a holder. Rejoin A and complete to match other side of neck.

SLEEVES

Using 3¼mm needles and A, cast on 36(38:40) sts. Work 5cm in K1, P1 rib as given for back, ending with a RS row. **Next row** Rib 4(5:6), M1, [rib 4, M1] to last 4(5:6) sts, rib to end. 44(46:48) sts. Change to 4mm needles. Beg K row, work 2 rows st st. Reading chart as given for front, set chart as folls: **Next row** With A, K11(12:13) sts, work 22 sts across 1st row of chart, with A, K to end. Cont in patt as set, at the same time inc one st at each end of every 4th(4th:5th) row, working in A only after 34 rows have been completed, until there are 76(78:80) sts. Cont without shaping until work measures 29(31:34)cm from beg, ending with a P row. Cast off.

COLLAR

Join shoulder seams. Using 3¼mm circular needle, A and with RS facing, start at centre front marker and K across 10(11:12) sts from right front holder, K up 14(15:16) sts up right front neck, K across 32(34:36) sts from back neck holder, K up 14(15:16) sts down left front neck and K across 10(11:12) sts from left front holder to centre front marker. 80(86:92) sts. Work 3 rounds K1, P1 rib, ending at centre front marker, inc one st at end of last round. 81(87:93) sts. Working backwards and forwards in rows, beg and ending K1 on every row, work 6cm K1, P1 rib. Cast off in rib.

TO MAKE UP

Press according to directions on ball band. With C embroider features onto Teddies using satin stitch for eyes and back stitch for nose and mouth, as in photograph. Place markers 15(16:17)cm down from shoulders on back and front. Sew in sleeves between markers. Join side and sleeve seams.

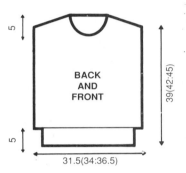

BACK AND FRONT
5
39(42:45)
5
31.5(34:36.5)

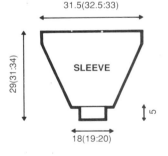

31.5(32.5:33)
29(31:34)
SLEEVE
5
18(19:20)

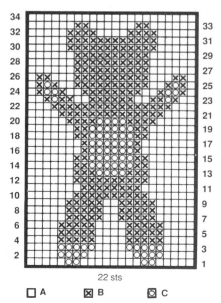

22 sts

□ A   ☒ B   ◉ C

Bow Sweater

A pretty raglan sleeve round-neck sweater with all-over bow motifs.

Skill Rating Experienced
Sizes To fit age 4(6:8) years
To fit chest 24(26:28)in/61(66:71)cm
Actual size 71(76:82)cm
Length to shoulder 43(44:46)cm *Sleeve seam* 28(29:31.5)cm
Materials 3(3:4) x 50g balls of 60% nylon/40% acrylic DK in
turquoise (colour A) and 1 ball same in white (B)
We used Patons Chantal DK
Pair each 3¼mm and 4mm knitting needles
4 buttons • 3mm crochet hook
Tension 22 sts and 30 rows to 10cm over st st on 4mm needles

BACK

Using 3¼mm needles and A, cast on 52 (58:64) sts. **1st and every row** [K1, P1] to end. Rep this row for 5(5:6)cm, ending with a RS row. **Next row** Rib 1(4:7), * M1, rib 2, rep from * to last 1(4:7) sts, M1, rib to end. 78(84:90) sts. Change to 4mm needles. Beg K row work 4(6:10) rows st st. Cont in patt from charts, reading odd-numbered (K) rows from right to left and even-numbered (P) rows from left to right. Use a separate ball of yarn for each area of colour and twist yarns together when changing colour to avoid a hole. Set position of patt as folls: **1st row** Work 12 sts across 1st row of chart 1, using A, K17(20:23) sts, work 21 sts across 1st row of chart 2, using A, K16(19:22) sts, work 12 sts across 1st row of chart 3. Cont working patt as set until 24 rows of charts have been completed. Using A only, work 10 rows st st. Set position of patt as folls: **Next row** Using A, K11(12:13) sts, work 21 sts across 1st row of chart 2, using A, K14(18:22) sts, work 21 sts across 1st row of chart 2 again, using A, K11(12:13) sts. Cont in patt as set until 24 rows of charts have been completed. Using A only, work 2 rows st st.

Shape raglans Cast off 2(3:4) sts at beg of next 2 rows, then dec one st each end of next and every foll alt row until 68(72:76) sts rem. P1 row. Set position of patt as folls: **Next row** Using A, dec one st, K22 (24:26) sts, work 21 sts across 1st row of chart 2, using A, K21(23:25) sts, dec one st. Cont in patt as set until row 24 of chart has been completed, at the same time cont to dec one st each end of foll alt rows **. Using A only, cont dec until 34(36:40) sts rem. Dec one st each end of every row until 18(20:22) sts rem, ending with a P row. Leave these sts on a holder.

FRONT

Work as given for back to **. Using A only, cont dec until 38(42:46) sts rem. P1 row.

Shape neck **Next row** K2 tog, K13(15: 17), turn and leave rem sts on a spare needle. **Next row** P2 tog, P to end. Cont to dec at neck and raglan edges on every alt row until 12(12:14) sts rem. Cont to dec at neck edge as before, but dec one st at raglan edge on every row until 3 sts rem. Work 1 more dec at raglan edge. P2 tog, fasten off. With RS facing, slip centre 8 sts onto a holder and complete as given for first side of neck.

SLEEVES

Using 3¼mm needles and A, cast on 38 sts and work 5(6:7)cm K1, P1 rib. **Next row** Rib 2, * M1, rib 2, rep from * to end. 56 sts. Change to 4mm needles. Beg K row, work 4(6:10) rows st st. Set position of patt as folls: **Next row** Using A, K17, work 21 sts across 1st row of chart 2, using A, K18. Cont in patt as set until row 24 of chart has been completed. Using A only, work 10 rows st st. Set position of patt as folls: **Next row** Work 12 sts across 1st row of chart 1, using A, K32 sts, work 12 sts across 1st row of chart 3. Cont in patt as set until row 24 of charts has been completed. Using A only, work 6 rows st st.

Shape raglans Cast off 3 sts at beg of next 2 rows. Dec one st each end of next row. 48 sts. P1 row. Set position of patt as folls: **Next row** Using A, dec one st, K11, work 21 sts across 1st row of chart 2, using A, K12, dec one st. Cont in patt as set, at

the same time dec one st at each end of every alt row until row 24 of chart has been completed. Using A only cont in st st, dec one st each end of every 3rd row until 8 sts rem, ending with a P row. Leave sts on a holder.

NECKBAND

Join front and right back raglan seams. Using 3¼mm needles, A and with RS facing, K across 8 sts of left sleeve, K up 13(15:17) sts down left front neck, K 8 sts from front neck holder, K up 13(15:17) sts up right front neck, K across 8 sts of right sleeve, K18(20:22) sts from back neck holder. 68(74:80) sts. Work 10 rows K1, P1 rib. Cast off loosely in rib.

TO MAKE UP

Join left back raglan seam, leaving 9cm open at top. Turn neckband in half to WS and slipstitch down. Join side and sleeve seams. Using 3mm crochet hook, work 1 row DC along sleeve edge of raglan opening, making 4 evenly spaced 6CH buttonholes. Sew on buttons.

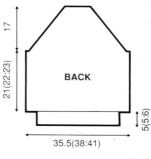

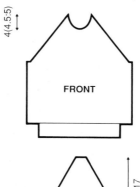

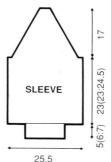

CHART 1

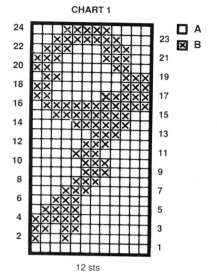

24
23
22
21
20
19
18
17
16
15
14
13
12
11
10
9
8
7
6
5
4
3
2
1

□ A
☒ B

12 sts

CHART 2

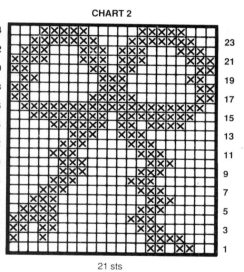

23
21
19
17
15
13
11
9
7
5
3
1

21 sts

CHART 3

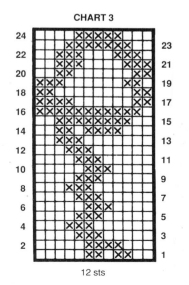

24
23
22
21
20
19
18
17
16
15
14
13
12
11
10
9
8
7
6
5
4
3
2
1

12 sts

Baseball Jacket

This simple stocking stitch jacket has the numbers 1, 2 and 3 and the letter B embroidered on afterwards using Swiss darning.

Skill Rating Medium
Sizes To fit age 6(8:10:12) years
To fit chest 26(28:30:32)in/66(71:76:81)cm
Actual size 71(76:82:86)cm
Length to shoulder 32(36:40:44)cm *Sleeve seam* 26(30:34:38)cm
Materials 4(4:5:5) x 50g balls of 80% wool/20% Bri-Nylon DK
in navy (colour A), 1(2:2:2) balls same in grey (B) and
1 ball same in each of gold (C), jade (D) and red (E)
We used Wendy Ascot DK
Pair each 3¾mm and 4mm knitting needles
6(7:7:7) buttons
Tension 24 sts and 32 rows to 10cm over st st on 4mm needles

BACK

Using 3¾mm needles and B, cast on 86 (90:98:102) sts. **1st rib row** K2, [P2, K2] to end. **2nd rib row** P2, [K2, P2] to end. Rep these 2 rows once more. With C rep these 2 rows twice. With B rep these 2 rows once then work 1st rib row again. *For 2nd and 4th sizes only* Inc in first st, rib as set to last 2 sts, inc in next st, rib last st. *For 1st and 3rd sizes* Work 2nd rib row. For all sizes 86(92:98:104) sts. Change to 4mm needles and A. Beg with a K row, cont in st st until work measures 12(13: 15:16)cm from beg, ending with a P row. With D work 4 rows. With B work 28(32: 36:40) rows. With D work 4 rows. With A cont until work measures 32(36:40:44)cm from beg, ending with a P row.
Shape shoulders Cast off 26(28:30:32) sts at beg of next 2 rows. Leave rem 34(36: 38:40) sts on a holder.

LEFT FRONT

Using 3¾mm needles and B cast on 46 (46:50:54) sts and work 5 rows K2, P2 rib in stripe patt as given for back.
Buttonhole row (WS) P1, P2 tog, cast on 2 sts, P2 tog, P1, rib to end. Cont until 11 rows of striped rib patt have been completed. **Next row** *2nd and 3rd sizes only* Inc in first st, rib as set to last 2 sts, inc in next st, rib last st. *1st and 4th sizes* Work 2nd rib row. *All sizes* 46(48:52:54) sts. Change to 4mm needles and A. **1st row** K to end, cast on 5 sts. 51(53:57:59) sts. **2nd row** P. Cont in st st for 8(10:12:14) rows. [**Buttonhole row** (RS)

K to last 10 sts, * K2 tog, cast on 2 sts, sl1, K1, psso *, K2, rep from * to *. Work 17(15:17:19) rows st st] 3(4:4:4) times. Rep buttonhole row again, work 10(10:14:16) rows st st. (For right front work 9(9:13:15) rows). Work measures 27(31:35:39)cm from beg.
Shape neck Cast off 16(16:17:17) sts at beg of next row. Dec one st at neck edge on next 9(9:10:10) rows. 26(28:30:32) sts. Cont without shaping until work measures same as back to shoulders, ending with a P row. Cast off.

RIGHT FRONT

Work to match left front noting bracketed exception and omitting buttonholes.

SLEEVES

Using 3¾mm needles and B, cast on 30 (34:38:38) sts and work 11 rows K2, P2 rib in stripe patt as given for back. Change to 4mm needles and A. Work 24(28:30:34) rows st st in A, then 4 rows rev st st in C, 28(32:36:40) rows st st in B, and 4 rows rev st st in C *at the same time* inc one st at each end of every foll 3rd(3rd:4th:4th) row. Then cont in st st with A, inc as before until there are 74(80:84:90) sts. Work straight until sleeve measures 26 (30:34:38)cm from beg, ending with a P row. Cast off.

POCKET

Using 3¾mm needles and B, cast on 26 (26:30:30) sts and work 11 rows K2, P2

rib in stripe patt as given for back. **Next row** Dec 1, [rib 5(5:6:6), dec 1] to last 2 sts, dec 1. 21(21:25:25) sts. Change to 4mm needles and A. Beg with a K row, cont in st st until work measures 10(10: 11:11)cm from beg. Cast off.

NECKBAND

Join shoulder seams. Fold 5 sts at edge of both fronts to inside of work, and slip stitch into place. Using 3¾mm needles, B and with RS facing, beg at folded edge and K up 29(30:31:32) sts up right front neck, K2(3:4:5), * M1, K6, rep from * to last 2(3:4:5) sts, M1, K to end, across back neck sts, K up 29(30:31:32) sts down left front neck. 98(102:106:110) sts. Beg P2, work 4 rows rib in stripe patt as given for back welt. **Next row** (WS) Work buttonhole row as given for left front welt. Cont until 11 rows of striped rib patt have been completed. Cast off in rib.

TO MAKE UP

Press according to directions on ball band. Place markers 15(16:17:19)cm down from shoulders on back and fronts. Sew in sleeves between markers. Join side and sleeve seams. Swiss Darn numbers and letter using charts as a guide. Work the letter B on right front using D and E. Work the number 2 on left sleeve using E, number 1 on right sleeve using D and number 3 on pocket using B. Sew pocket on to left front. Sew on buttons.

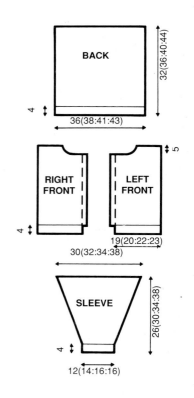

Alpine Daisy Cardigan

Any little girl will love this Heidi-style cardigan scattered with daisies.

Skill Rating Easy
Sizes To fit age 2(4:6:8:10) years
To fit chest 22(24:26:28:30)in/56(61:66:71:76)cm
Actual size 67(72:76:80:86)cm
Length to shoulder 38(41:44:49:51)cm *Sleeve seam* 24(29:35:41:42)cm
Materials 6(6:7:7:8) x 50g balls of 100% wool DK in scarlet (colour A),
1 ball same in black (B) and oddment in white (C)
We used Sunbeam Pure New Wool DK
Pair each of 3¼mm and 4mm knitting needles • 6 buttons
Tension 21 sts and 40 rows to 10cm over moss st on 4 mm needles

BACK

Using 4mm needles and A, cast on 67(73: 77:83:89) sts. **Moss st row** K1, [P1, K1] to end. Rep moss st row until work measures 25(27:29:33:34)cm from beg.

Shape armholes Cast off 2 sts at beg of next 2 rows. Dec one st at each end of every row until 51(57:61:67:73) sts rem. Cont without shaping until work measures 38(41:44: 49:51)cm from beg.

Shape shoulders In patt cast off 7(8:8:9:10) sts at beg of next 2 rows and 6(7:8:9:10) sts at beg of foll 2 rows. Leave rem 25(27:29:31:33) sts on a holder.

LEFT FRONT

Using 4mm needles and A, cast on 35(37: 39:43:45) sts. Work in moss st as given for back until front measures same as back to armholes.

Shape armhole Cast off 2 sts at beg of next row. Dec one st at armhole edge on every row until 27(29:31:35:37) sts rem. Cont without shaping until front measures 5cm less than back to shoulder, ending at front edge.

Shape neck Cast off 6(6:7:8:8) sts at beg of next row. Dec one st at neck edge on every row until 13(15:16:18:20) sts rem. Work without shaping until front matches back to shoulder, ending at armhole edge.

Shape shoulder Cast off 7(8:8:9:10) sts at beg of next row. Work 1 row. Cast off rem 6(7:8:9:10) sts

RIGHT FRONT

Work as given for left front.

SLEEVES

Using 4mm needles and A, cast on 37(39: 43:45:47) sts. Work 10cm in moss st. Cont in moss st, inc one st at each end of 3rd (5th:3rd:5th:7th) and every foll 4th(4th: 6th:6th:6th) row until there are 59(63: 67:71:75) sts. Cont straight until sleeve measures 29(34:40:46:47)cm from beg.

Shape top Cast off 2 sts at beg of next 2 rows. Dec one st at each end of every row until 43(47:51:55:59) sts rem. Cast off 8 sts at beg of next 4 rows. Cast off rem 11(15:19:23:27) sts.

NECKBAND

Join shoulder seams. With RS of work facing, 3¼mm needles and A, K up 28(28:29:30:30) sts up right front neck, inc in first and last st K across 25(27:29: 31:33) sts of back neck, K up 28(28:29: 30:30) sts down left front neck. 83(85:89: 93:95) sts. **1st rib row** (WS) P1, [K1, P1] to end. **2nd rib row** K1, [P1, K1] to end. Rep these 2 rows once, then work 1st row again. With B, K 1 row. Cast off in rib.

BUTTONHOLE BAND

With RS of right front facing and 3¼mm needles, K up 99(105:111:117:121) sts in A and 2 sts in B evenly between lower edge and cast-off edge of neckband, working 2 sts in B to correspond with edge of neckband. 101(107:113:119:123) sts. **1st rib row** (WS) With B, K1, P1, twist A and B tog to prevent a hole, then with A, K1, [P1, K1] to end. **2nd rib row** With A, rib to last 2 sts, twist yarns, rib 2 B.

Rep 1st rib row. Working 2 sts at neck edge in B on every row, cont thus: **1st buttonhole row** Rib 2(2:3:3:3), [cast off next 2 sts, rib until there are 17 (18:19:20:21) sts on right needle after cast-off sts] 5 times, cast off next 2 sts, rib to end. **2nd buttonhole row** Rib to end casting on 2 sts over each cast-off group. With B, K 1 row. Cast off in rib.

BUTTON BAND

Working 2 sts in B at neck edge on every row, work as buttonhole band, omitting buttonholes.

TO MAKE UP

Join side and sleeve seams, reversing seam on lower 7cm of sleeve for cuff. Set in sleeves. Sew on buttons.

Using lazy daisy stitch and French knots, work embroidery on fronts using B and C as shown. Turn lower 5cm of sleeves onto RS.

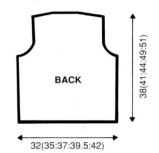

BACK
38(41:44:49:51)
32(35:37:39.5:42)

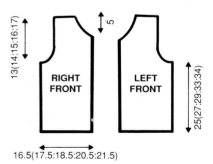

RIGHT FRONT
LEFT FRONT
13(14:15:16:17)
5
25(27:29:33:34)
16.5(17.5:18.5:20.5:21.5)

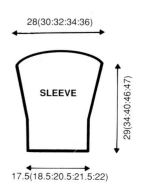

28(30:32:34:36)
SLEEVE
29(34:40:46:47)
17.5(18.5:20.5:21.5:22)

Contrast Cardigan

A cotton cardigan knitted in a simple all-over pattern with Fair Isle borders.

Skill Rating Medium
Sizes To fit age 6(8:10) years
To fit chest 26(28:30)in/66(71:76)cm
Actual size 71(76:81)cm
Length to shoulder 42(46:50)cm *Sleeve seam* 33(36:38)cm
Materials 6(6:7) x 50g balls of 100% cotton DK in turquoise (colour A)
and 2 balls same in yellow (B)
We used Patons Laguna
Pair each 3mm and 4mm knitting needles • 8 buttons
Tension 24 sts and 27 rows to 10cm over st st on 4mm needles

BACK

Using 3mm needles and A, cast on 75(79:85) sts. **1st rib row** (RS) K1, [P1, K1] to end. **2nd rib row** P1, [K1, P1] to end. Rep these 2 rows for 5(6:6)cm, ending with a 1st rib row. **Next row** (WS) Rib 10(6:9), * inc in next st, rib 5, rep from * to last 11 7:10) sts, inc in next st, rib to end. 85(91:97) sts. Change to 4mm needles. Cont in patt beg at size indicated on chart, reading odd-numbered (K) rows from right to left and even-numbered (P) rows from left to right. Strand yarn not in use loosely across WS. Work 22 rows of chart then rep 11th-22nd rows until work measures 42(46:50)cm from beg, ending with a WS row.
Shape shoulders **Next row** Cast off 29(31:34) sts, patt until there are 27(29:29) sts on right hand needle, cast off rem 29(31:34) sts. Leave rem 27(29:29) sts on a holder.

LEFT FRONT

Using 3mm needles and A, cast on 33(35:37) sts. Work 5(6:6)cm K1, P1 rib as given for back, ending with a 1st rib row. **Next row** Rib 6(4:7), * inc in next st, rib 2(2:1), rep from * to last 6(4:8) sts, inc in next st, rib to end. 41(45:49) sts. Change to 4mm needles. Cont in patt beg at size indicated on chart. Work 22 rows of chart then rep 11th-22nd rows until work measures 34(38:42)cm from beg, ending with a RS row (for right front end with a WS row).
Shape neck Cast off 4 sts at beg of next row. Dec one st at neck edge on next 1(6:7) rows, then on every foll alt row until 29(31:34) sts rem. Cont straight until front matches back to shoulder, ending with a WS row. Cast off.

RIGHT FRONT

Work to match left front.

SLEEVES

Using 3mm needles and A, cast on 37(39:41) sts. Work 3(4:4)cm K1, P1 rib as given for back, ending with a 1st rib row. **Next row** Rib 7(6:5), * inc in next st, rib 1, rep from * to last 8(7:6) sts, inc in next st, rib to end. 49(53:57) sts. Change to 4mm needles. Cont in patt from chart beg as indicated for 3rd(1st:3rd) size of back, at the same time, inc one st at each end of 5th and every foll 4th row until there are 83(91:97) sts. Cont without further shaping until sleeve measures 33(36:38)cm from beg, ending with a WS row. Cast off.

BUTTON BAND

Using 3mm needles and B, cast on 7 sts. Work K1, P1 rib as given for back until band is long enough, when slightly stretched, to fit up left front to neck edge, ending with a 1st rib row (for buttonhole band, end 2nd rib row). **Next row** Cast off 4 sts and sl rem 3 sts on to a safety pin. Sew button band on to left front. Mark the positions of 8 buttons, the first 1.5cm from lower edge, the last 1.5cm below neck edge and the rem 6 evenly spaced between.

BUTTONHOLE BAND

Work to match button band making buttonholes opposite markers as folls:
Buttonhole row (RS) Rib 3, yon, K2 tog, rib to end. Sew buttonhole band onto right front.

COLLAR

Join shoulder seams. Using 3mm needles, B and with RS facing, rib across 3 sts of buttonhole band, K up 23 sts up right front neck, K across 27(29:29) back neck sts, K up 23 sts down left front neck and rib across 3 sts of button band. 79(81:81) sts. Beg with a 2nd rib row cont in K1, P1 rib as given for back for 2cm. Change to 4mm needles and cont in rib until collar measures 8(9:10)cm from beg. Cast off in rib.

TO MAKE UP

Press according to directions on ball band. Place a marker 17(19:20)cm down from shoulders on back and fronts. Sew sleeves between markers. Join side and sleeve seams. Sew on buttons.

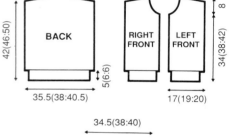

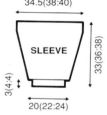

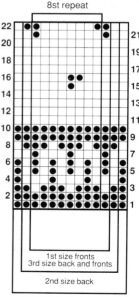

	A			B

Goosey Goosey Gander Sweater

Fair Isle geese make an all over pattern on this classic sweater. Eyes, legs and beaks are Swiss darned.

Skill Rating Experienced
Sizes To fit age 2(4:6:8:10) years
To fit chest 22(24:26:28:30)in/56(61:66:71:76)cm
Actual size 65(70:76:81:86)cm
Length to shoulder 36(40:43:49:53)cm *Sleeve seam* 26(29:32:35:38)cm
Materials 4(4:5:5:6) x 50g balls of 100% wool DK in blue (colour A), 2(2:2:3:3)
balls same in white (B) and 1 ball same in yellow (C)
We used Emu Superwash DK
Pair each 3¼mm and 4½mm knitting needles
Tension 23 sts and 23 rows to 10cm over patt on 4½mm needles

BACK

Using 3¼mm needles and A, cast on 65 (71:77:83:89) sts. **1st rib row** K1, [P1, K1] to end. **2nd rib row** P1, [K1, P1] to end. Rep these 2 rows for 5cm, ending with a 1st rib row. **Next row** Rib 5(4:7:5:8), * M1, rib 6(7:7:8:8), rep from * to last 6(4:7:6:9) sts, M1, rib to end. 75(81:87:93:99) sts. Change to 4½mm needles. Cont in patt from chart reading odd-numbered (K) rows from right to left and even-numbered (P) rows from left to right. Strand B when not in use loosely across WS. Beg and ending at size indicated, work sts before dotted line, work 26 st rep twice, work sts beyond dotted line **. Cont in patt until 72(80:88:102:110) chart rows from beg have been completed.
Shape shoulders Cast off 25(27:29:31: 33) sts at beg of next 2 rows. Leave rem 25(27:29:31:33) sts on a holder.

FRONT

Work as given for back to **. Cont in patt until 54(62:72:80:90) chart rows from beg have been completed.
Shape neck **Next row** Patt 32(34:36:38: 40) sts, turn and leave rem sts on a spare needle. Keeping patt correct, dec one st at neck edge on next 4 rows then on every alt row until 25(27:29:31:33) sts rem. Cont without shaping until front matches back to shoulder, ending at side edge. Cast off. With RS facing, slip centre 11(13:15:17:19) sts on to a holder, rejoin yarn and complete to match other side of neck.

SLEEVES

Using 3¼mm needles and A, cast on 31 (35:39:43:47) sts. **1st rib row** (RS) K1,[P1, K1] to end. **2nd rib row** P1, [K1, P1] to end. Rep these 2 rows for 5cm, ending with a 1st rib row. **Next row** (WS) Rib 2(4:6:3:5), * M1, rib 3(3:3:4:4), rep from * to last 2(4:6:4:6) sts, M1, rib to end. 41(45:49:53:57) sts. Change to 4½mm needles. Beg with a K row, cont in st st and patt from chart beg and ending at size indicated, at the same time, inc one st at each end of 3rd and every foll 3rd(3rd: 4th:4th:5th) row until there are 69(73:77: 81:85) sts, taking inc sts into patt. Cont without shaping until sleeve measures 26(29:32:35:38)cm from beg, ending with a WS row. Cast off loosely with A.

NECKBAND

Join right shoulder seam. Using 3¼mm needles, A and with RS facing, K up 20 sts down left front neck, K across 11(13:15: 17:19) centre front sts, K up 20 sts up right front neck and K across 25(27:29:31:33) back neck sts on holder. 76(80:84:88:92) sts. Work 5cm in K1, P1 rib. Cast off loosely in rib.

TO MAKE UP

Press according to directions on ball band. Join left shoulder and neckband seam. Fold neckband in half to WS and slip stitch loosely in position. Place markers 15(16: 17:17:5:18.5)cm down from shoulders on back and front. Sew in sleeves between markers. Join side and sleeve seams. Swiss darn eyes, legs and beaks with C (yellow) following chart.

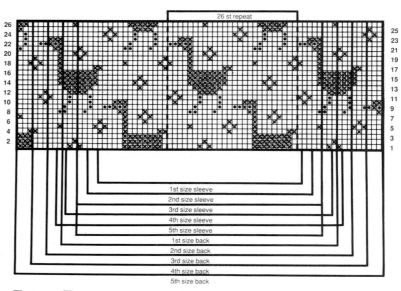

☐ A   ☒ B   ⊙ Work in A or B as appropriate, Swiss darn afterwards

Sailor Suits

Easy-to-knit nautical numbers that the little ones will love.

Skill Rating Easy
Sizes To fit age 1-2(2-3:3-4) years
To fit chest 21(22:23)in/53(56:59)cm
Actual chest measurement 58(61.5:65)cm
Playsuit: Length 49(57:65)cm *Sleeve seam* 6(8:10)cm *Jumper: Length* 32(37:42)cm
Sleeve seam 18(21:23)cm *Shorts: Length* 29(33:37)cm
Materials Playsuit 3(4:5) x 50g balls of 100% cotton DK in navy (colour A)
and 3(3:4) balls same in white (B)
Jumper 4(5:6) balls same in navy (colour A) and 1 ball white (B)
Shorts 3(3:4) balls same in white (B)
We used Patons Laguna DK
Pair of 4mm knitting needles • 5 buttons for back of playsuit
4 buttons for shoulders of playsuit • 4 buttons for jumper
Waist length of 2·5cm wide elastic for shorts
Tension 22 sts and 30 rows to 10cm over st st on 4mm needles

PLAYSUIT

BACK

First leg With A cast on 26(27:28) sts. Work 4 rows g st. Cont in st st, inc one st at beg of 5th(3rd:1st and 7th) rows, work 8 rows. Working in stripes of 12 rows B and 12 rows A, inc one st at beg of 3rd (1st:5th) row and every foll 6th row until there are 31(33:35) sts. Inc one st at shaped edge on next 5 rows. 36(38:40) sts *. Leave sts on a spare needle.

Second leg Working inc sts at end of rows instead of at beg, work as for first leg to *. **Next row** K36(38:40), cast on 2(4:6), K36(38:40) sts of first leg. 74(80:86) sts. Cont in stripes, work 25(29:33) rows. Dec one st at each end of next and every foll 4th row until 64(68:72) sts rem **. P1 row, ending with 10th row of stripe worked in A(B:A).

Make buttonholes **Next row** K9(11:13), [yo, K2 tog, K9] 4 times, yo, K2 tog, K9(11:13). Work 4 rows g st. Cast off.

Top of back With A(B:A) cast on 68(72:76) sts. Work 4 rows g st. Dec one st at each end of 3rd and 7th rows, st st 10 rows. *** Cont in 12 row stripes, work 64(76:88) rows.

Shape shoulders **Next row** K20(21:22), turn and cast off these sts knitwise. Cast off centre 24(26:28) sts, K to end. Cast off 20(21:22) sts knitwise.

FRONT

Work as given for back to **. Work as for back from *** until 4 rows less than back to shoulder have been worked.

Shape neck **Next row** K 23(24:25), turn and complete left side of neck on these sts. Dec one st at neck edge on next 3 rows. Cast off. Cast off centre 18(20:22) sts, K to end. Complete right side of neck to match left side.

Neck edging With RS facing, join A to 7th(8th:9th) cast-off st of left shoulder, K up 13 sts from rem shoulder, 28(30:32) sts around front neck and 13 sts from first 13 cast-off sts of right shoulder. 54(56:58) sts. K1 row.

Make buttonholes **Next row** K3, * yo, K2 tog, K4, yo, K2 tog *, K to last 11 sts, rep from * to *, K3. K1 row. Cast off knitwise.

SLEEVES

With B(A:B) cast on 46(50:54) sts. Work 4 rows g st. Inc one st at each end of 1st and every foll 4th row, cont in st st work 8 rows B(A:B), then cont in 12 row stripes until there are 54(60:66) sts. Work 1(3:5) rows. Cast off.

COLLAR

With B cast on 52(58:64) sts. Work 4 rows g st. Cont in st st with g st borders. **1st row** (RS) K. **2nd row** K 2(3:4), P to last 2(3:4) sts, K2(3:4). Rep last 2 rows 10(11:12) times. **Next row** K. **Next row** K2(3:4), P9, K30(34:38), P9, K2(3:4). Rep last 2 rows once. **Next row** K13(15:17), turn, cont on these sts only for right side of collar. **1st row** K2(3:4), P9, K2(3:4). **2nd row** K. Rep last 2 rows twice, then work

1st row again. **8th row** K to last 4(6:8) sts, K2 tog, K2(4:6). **9th row** K2(3:4), P to last 2(3:4) sts, K2(3:4). **10th row** K2(3:4), M1, K to last 4(5:6) sts, K2 tog, K2(3:4). **11th row** As 9th. Rep last 4 rows until 5(7:9) sts rem. Work 12 rows g st. K3 tog at centre of next and every foll 4th row until 3 sts rem, K3 tog and fasten off. With right side facing cast off centre 26(28:30) sts, K to end. Complete left side of collar as given for right, reversing shapings and working skpo instead of K2 tog.

Make loop Cast on 7 sts. K 27 rows. Cast off. Join ends.

POCKET

With B cast on 19 sts. Work 24 rows st st. Work 4 rows g st. Cast off.

TO MAKE UP

Lap back buttonhole band over first stripe of top, secure ends, sew on buttons. Join leg seams. Join outer ends of shoulders. Lap front neck edging over back and secure outer ends. Sew on buttons. Place markers 12(13.5:15)cm down from shoulders. Sew sleeves between markers. Join side and sleeve seams. With A, Swiss darn anchor motif. Sew on pocket. Sew centre cast-off edge of collar to back neck, take pointed ends to front, slip through loop and secure.

JUMPER

BACK

With A cast on 64(68:72) sts. Work 4 rows g st. Cont in st st work 4(8:12) rows A, 6 rows B, 6 rows A and 6 rows B. Cont in A, work 70(82:94) rows.

Shape shoulders Work as given for back of playsuit.

FRONT

Work as back until 4 rows less than back to shoulder shaping have been worked. Shape neck and work neck edging as front of playsuit.

SLEEVES

With A cast on 30(32:34) sts. Work 4 rows g st. While working st st stripes of [6 rows A and 6 rows B] twice, then working in A only, inc one st at each end of 3rd and every foll 4th row until there are 54(60:66) sts. Work 3(3:1) rows straight. Cast off. Work collar in B and pocket with A, as given for playsuit.

TO MAKE UP

Join seams. Sew on collar. Reversing colours of chart, embroider and sew on pocket as for playsuit.

SHORTS

BACK AND FRONT

Both alike Using B throughout, work as for playsuit to **. Cont in st st, work 7 rows. **Eyelet row** K2, [yo, K2 tog] to end. St st 7 rows. Cast off.

TO MAKE UP

Join seams. Join elastic in a ring. Fold waist to WS at eyelet row and sew down, enclosing elastic.

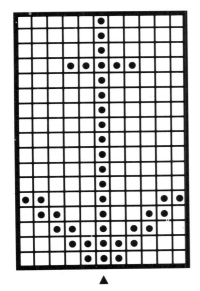

▲
centre st

▣ A   ☐ B

Clown Face Sweater

A brightly coloured picture sweater in double knitting wool. The sleeves are trimmed with a diamond patterned Fair Isle band.

Skill Rating Experienced
Sizes To fit age 6 months (1:2:4) years
To fit chest 18(20:22:24)in/46(51:56:61)cm
Actual size 56(62:66:70)cm
Length to shoulder 37(39:41:43)cm *Sleeve seam* 20(23:25:28)cm
Materials 5(5:5:6) x 50g balls of 100% wool DK in pink (colour A),
1 ball same in each of yellow (B), green (C), turquoise (D),
red (E), orange (F), black (G), white (H) and purple (J)
We used Emu Superwash DK
Pair each 3¼mm and 4mm knitting needles • 3 buttons
Tension 22 sts and 30 rows to 10cm over st st on 4mm needles

BACK

* Using 3¼mm needles and A, cast on 61(67:71:77) sts. **1st rib row** K1, [P1, K1] to end. **2nd rib row** P1, [K1, P1] to end. Rep these 2 rows for 5cm, ending with a 1st rib row. **Next row** Rib 31(34:36:39), M1, rib as set to end. 62(68:72:78) sts *. Change to 4mm needles and cont in st st until work measures 28(30:32:34)cm from beg, ending with a P row.

Divide for opening **Next row** K33(36:38:41) sts, turn and leave rem sts on a spare needle. **1st row** K4, P to end. **2nd row** K. **3rd row** K4, P to end. **Buttonhole row** K to last 3 sts, yon, K2 tog, K1. Rep 1st and 2nd rows 5 times more, then work 1st row again. Work buttonhole row. Rep 1st and 2nd rows 4 times more, then work 1st row again, so ending at side edge.

Shape shoulder Cast off 10(11:12:13) sts at beg of next row and 10(11:11:12) sts at beg of foll alt row. Leave rem 13(14:15:16) sts on a holder. With A cast on 4 sts, then with RS facing, K rem sts from spare needle. 33(36:38:41) sts. Complete to match first side of neck, omitting buttonholes and reversing shoulder shaping.

FRONT

Work as given for back from * to *. Change to 4mm needles and work 2(6:12:16) rows st st in A, ending with a P row. Cont in st st and patt from chart 1, reading odd-numbered (K) rows from right to left and even-numbered (P) rows from left to right. Use a separate ball of yarn for each area of colour and twist

yarns tog on WS when changing colour to avoid a hole. Cont in patt until 70 chart rows have been completed, so ending with a P row.

Shape neck **Next row** Patt 24(27:29:32), K2 tog, turn and leave rem sts on a spare needle. Keeping chart patt correct, dec one st at neck edge on next 3 rows, then dec one st at neck edge on foll 2 alt rows. 20(23:25:28) sts. 78 chart rows have now been completed. Cont in A only, dec one st at neck edge on foll 0(1:2:3) alt rows. 20(22:23:25) sts. Cont without shaping until front matches back to shoulder, ending at side edge.

Shape shoulder Cast off 10(11:12:13) sts at beg of next row. Work 1 row. Cast off rem 10(11:11:12) sts. With RS facing, sl centre 10 sts onto a holder, rejoin A, K2 tog, K to end. Complete to match first side of neck working in A only.

SLEEVES

Using 3¼mm needles and A, cast on 33(35:37:39) sts. Work 4.5cm in rib as given for back, ending with a 1st rib row. **Next row** (WS) Rib 5(2:3:3), * M1, rib 3(4:4:4), rep from * to last 4(1:2:4) sts, M1, rib to end. 42(44:46:48) sts. Change to 4mm needles and cont in st st, inc one st at each end of 5th row. 44(46:48:50) sts. Work 3 more rows, then work 15 rows of chart 2 starting at point indicated for size, reading 1st and all RS (K) rows from right to left, 2nd and all WS (P) rows from left to right, stranding colour not in use loosely on WS of work, at the same time inc one st at each end of 5th and foll 4th rows twice as shown on chart. 50(52:54:56) sts. Complete chart 2, then

cont in A only, inc one st at each end of every foll 3rd(3rd:4th:4th) row from previous inc until there are 68(70:72:74) sts. Cont without shaping until sleeve measures 20(23:25:28)cm from beg, ending with a P row. Cast off loosely.

NECKBAND

Join shoulder seams. With 3¼mm needles, A and with RS of work facing, K across 13(14:15:16) sts of left back neck, K up 18(20:22:24) sts down left front neck, K across 10 front neck sts, K up 18(20:22:24) sts up right front neck, then K across 13(14:15:16) sts from right back neck. 72(78:84:90) sts. K3 rows.

Buttonhole row K to last 5 sts, K2 tog, yon, K3. K 2 more rows. Cast off loosely.

TO MAKE UP

Place markers 15.5(16:16.5:17)cm down from shoulders on back and front. Sew in sleeves between markers. Join side and sleeve seams. Sew on buttons. Embroider outline of eyebrows in stem stitch with G, as shown by curved lines on chart 1.

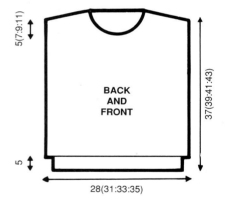

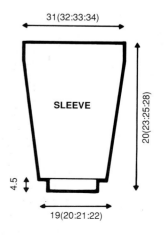

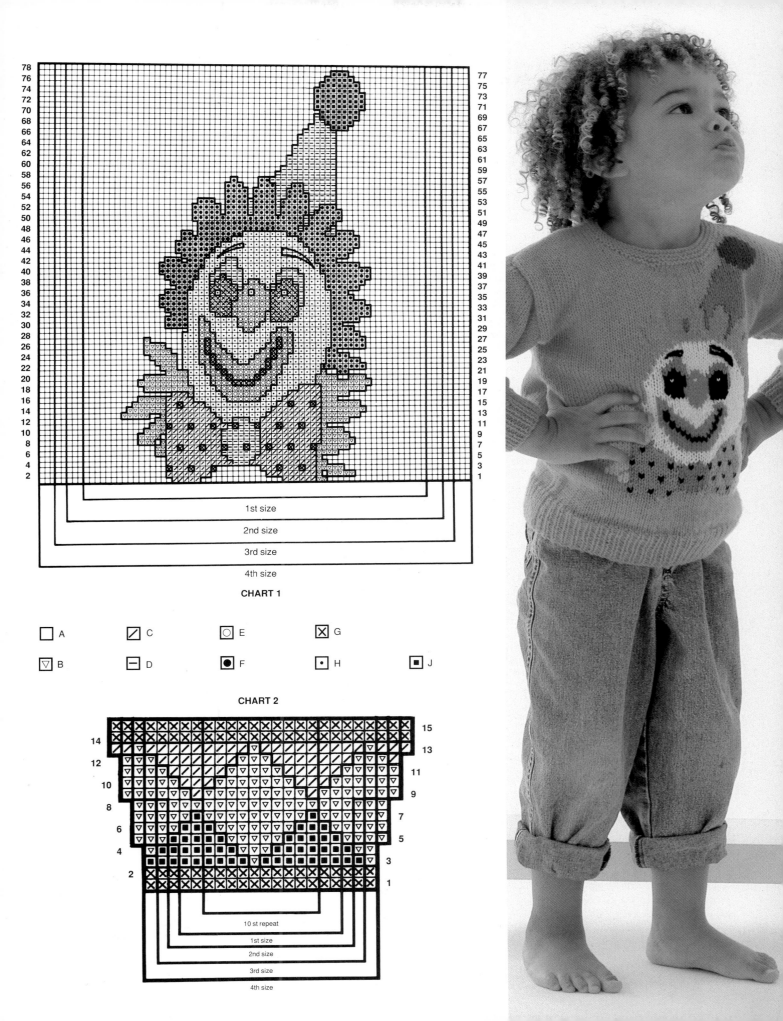

CHART 1

1st size
2nd size
3rd size
4th size

A   C   E   G

B   D   F   H   J

CHART 2

10 st repeat
1st size
2nd size
3rd size
4th size

Christmas Holly Sweater

A brightly coloured sweater with holly leaves and bows. Small bobbles form the three-dimensional holly berries.

Skill Rating Experienced
Sizes To fit age 4(6:8) years
To fit chest 24(26:28)in/61(66:71)cm
Actual size 79(84:90)cm
Length to shoulder 40(46:49)cm *Sleeve seam* 27(31:35)cm
Materials 4(5:5) x 50g balls of 45% acrylic/40% Bri-Nylon/15% wool DK in red (colour A), 1 ball same in dark green (B) and 1 ball same in mid green (C)
We used Hayfield Grampian DK
Pair each of 3¼mm and 4mm knitting needles
A 3¼mm circular needle, 40 cm long
Tension 22 sts and 28 rows to 10cm over st st on 4mm needles
Special Abbreviation
mb = make bobble on RS thus: K1, P1, K1, P1 in next st, turn, K4, turn, P4, turn, (K2 tog) twice, turn, K2 tog. Make bobble on WS thus: K1, P1, K1, P1 in next st, turn, P4, turn, K4, turn, (P2 tog) twice, turn, P2 tog, push bobble to RS

BACK

* Using 3¼mm needles and B, cast on 68(74:80) sts. **1st row** Using B, [K1, P1] to end. **2nd row** Using A, P to end. **3rd to 10th rows** using A, [K1, P1] to end. **11th row** Using C, K to end. **12th row** Using C, rib to end. **13th row** Using A, K to end. **14th to 18th rows** Using A, rib to end. **Next row** Using A, rib 4(7:10), [inc in next st, rib 2] 20 times, inc in next st, rib 3(6:9). 89(95:101) sts. Change to 4mm needles. Beg with a P row, cont in st st until work measures 15(20:22)cm, ending with a P row. Cont in patt from chart 1 (see page 96), reading odd-numbered (K) rows from right to left and even-numbered (P) rows from left to right. Use a separate ball of yarn for each area of colour and twist yarns tog when changing colour to avoid a hole *. When 70 rows of chart have been completed cont in A only and work 0(4:6) rows st st.
Shape shoulders Cast off 16(17:18) sts at beg of next 4 rows. Leave rem 25(27:29) sts on a spare needle.

FRONT

Work as given for back from * to *. Complete 58(62:64) rows of chart.
Shape neck **Next row** Patt 38(40:42) sts, turn and leave rem sts on a spare needle. Dec one st at neck edge on every row until 32(34:36) sts rem. Cont without shaping until front matches back to shoulder, ending at side edge.
Shape shoulder Cast off 16(17:18) sts at beg of next row. Work 1 row. Cast off rem 16(17:18) sts. With RS facing, slip centre 13(15:17) sts on to a spare needle, marking centre st with contrast colour thread. Rejoin yarn to rem sts and patt to end. Complete as given for other side of neck.

SLEEVES

Using 3¼mm needles and B, cast on 36(38:40) sts. **1st row** Using B, [K1, P 1] to end. **2nd row** Using A, P to end. **3rd to 6th rows** Using A, [K1, P1] to end. **7th row** Using C, K to end. **8th row** Using C, rib to end. **9th row** Using A, K to end. **10th to 13th rows** Using A, rib to end. **Next row** Using A, rib 4(5:6), [inc in next st, rib 1] 14 times, rib 4(5:6). 50(52:54) sts. Change to 4mm needles and working in st st cont in patt from chart 2 (see page 96), reading odd-numbered (K) rows from right to left and even-numbered (P) rows from left to right. At the same time inc one st at each end of 5th and every foll 6th row until chart is complete, then cont in A until there are 64(68:72) sts, taking inc sts into patt. Cont without shaping until sleeve measures 27(31:35)cm, ending with a P row. Cast off loosely.

COLLAR

Join shoulder seams. Using 3¼mm circular needle and A, K up 16(17:18) sts down left side of neck, 13(15:17) sts from centre front inc 2 sts evenly across, 16(17:18) sts up right side of neck, 25(27:29) sts from centre back, inc 4 sts evenly across. 76(82:88) sts. Work 4 rounds K1, P1 rib. Work in rib to within st before centre front marker, inc in next st. 77(83:89) sts. Turn and work 6 rows backwards and forwards in K1, P1 rib. **Next row** Using C, K to end. **Next row** Using C, rib to end. **Next row** Using A, K to end. Using A, rib 8 more rows. **Next row** Using C, P to end. **Next row** Using C, rib to end. Cast off loosely with C.

TO MAKE UP

Mark position of armholes 14.5(15.5: 16.5)cm down from shoulders on back and front. Sew in sleeves between markers. Join side and sleeve seams.

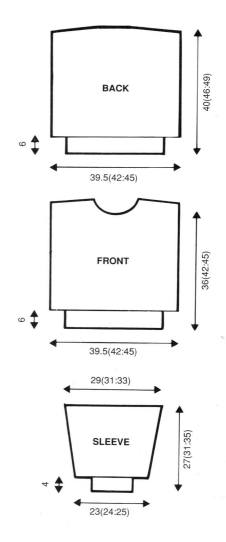

BACK
40(46:49)
6
39.5(42:45)

FRONT
36(42:45)
6
39.5(42:45)

29(31:33)
SLEEVE
27(31:35)
4
23(24:25)

CHART 1

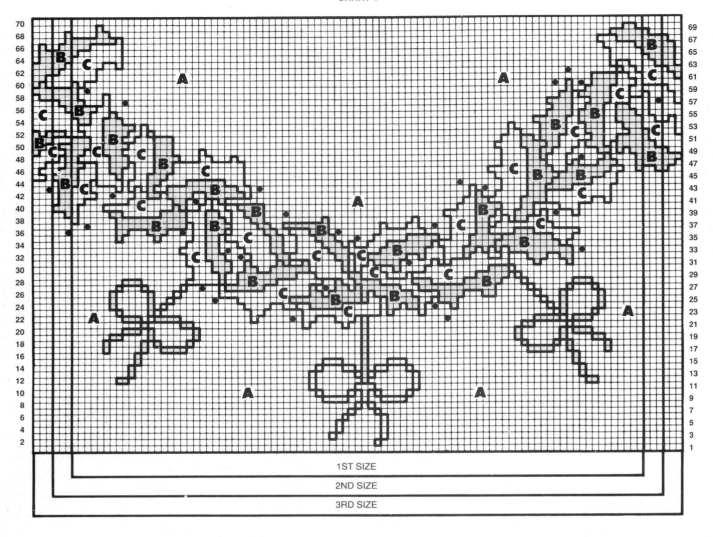

1ST SIZE

2ND SIZE

3RD SIZE

CHART 2

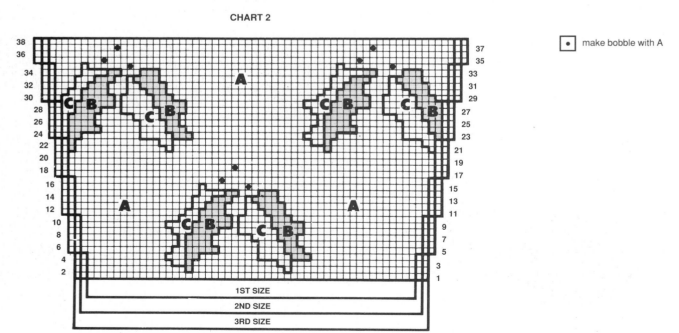

1ST SIZE

2ND SIZE

3RD SIZE

· make bobble with A